THE SCIENTIFIC EXAMINATION OF RELIGION

*Edited by Tom Flynn, Ronald A. Lindsay,
Andrea Szalanski, and Julia Lavarnway*

The Best of
FREE INQUIRY

INQUIRY PRESS
Amherst, NY

The Best of Free Inquiry:
THE SCIENTIFIC EXAMINATION OF RELIGION

©2013 INQUIRY PRESS
Center for Inquiry, Inc.
PO Box 741, Amherst, NY 14226-0741
Phone: 716-636-4869 • Fax: 716-636-1733
All rights reserved.

Printed in USA

ISBN-10: 1937998010
ISBN-13: 978-1-937998-01-1

The articles in this book first appeared in
Free Inquiry, the flagship magazine of
the Council for Secular Humanism.

CONTENTS

THE SCIENTIFIC EXAMINATION OF RELIGION

INTRODUCTION
Tom Flynn

This book is the second in an ongoing series that brings together selected articles that appeared in *Free Inquiry* magazine between 2000 and 2012. If you're unfamiliar with *Free Inquiry*, it is the flagship journal of the Council for Secular Humanism, generally recognized (modesty aside) as one of the humanist/atheist/freethought movement's premier magazines in English. If you're wondering why I had to set modesty aside, I have had the honor of editing *Free Inquiry* during the years this anthology encompasses. The purpose of this series of books is, then, to bring together some of the best and most significant writing that has brightened the pages of *Free Inquiry* during my tenure as editor.

A great number of articles appeared over twelve years, especially given that *Free Inquiry* switched from quarterly to bimonthly publication in the fall of 2003. When we editors revisited that body of articles, we came away with enough "best-of-class" articles to fill six anthologies. The series will be arranged by topic. The previous volume, *Secular Humanism and Its Commitments*, focused on secular humanism's purpose, function, and distinctive stances. This volume focuses on secular humanism's examination and critique of religion. Future volumes will focus on the harm done by religion, secularization and the West, secular humanism and public policy, and secular humanism and future trends.

The title of this volume is *The Scientific Examination of Religion*. Religious institutions and scholars have often claimed to stand above scientific scrutiny, using "science" in the broad sense to connote not only the familiar physical sciences but also such scholarly disciplines as history, sociology, philology, linguistics, and archaeology. On one religious view, the things of God are not subject to review by any merely human discipline. The Council for Secular Humanism, *Free Inquiry*'s publisher, has rejected that stance—and has, since the dawn of its organizational history, put that refusal into action.

The Council for Democratic and Secular Humanism (as it was then called) was not yet two years old when *Free Inquiry*'s cover featured "A Call for the Critical Examination of the Bible and Religion" (*FI*, Spring 1982). In those days critically important documents would actually have their texts begin on the cover; that had been done with "A Secular Humanist Declaration" in *FI*'s premier issue, and it was done again here. *FI* founder Paul Kurtz, Fellowship of Religious Humanists president Paul Beattie, famed philosopher Sidney Hook, ethicist Joseph Fletcher, historian Gerald Larue, and philosopher Richard Taylor cosigned the document, urging revival of a "powerful rational analysis of religion that developed from the eighteenth century through the first two decades of the twentieth." That analysis, the cosigners charged, "has been dissipated by various forms of neo-orthodoxy" . . . a "new obscurantism" in consequence of which "the public is largely unaware" about what scholarship had *already* revealed about the true origins and import of the world's religious traditions.

In April 1982, *Free Inquiry* held its first national conference at the State University of New York at Buffalo's Amherst campus, immediately adjacent to the present location of the Center for Inquiry–Transnational, *FI*'s headquarters. There, scholars under the direction of Gerald Larue, Robert Alley, and others formed the Religion and Biblical Criticism Research Project, in part "to disseminate the many investigations carried on over the past century" by "Jewish and Christian scholars" that "have not been shared with the public" (*FI*, Fall 1982).

Let's unpack these statements. Starting in the late 1700s, a slow-motion explosion of scholarly research into the origins of Christianity and the Bible revolutionized the way Christian intellectuals in Europe understood their faith. By the early twentieth century, Protestant scholars all knew—and most Protestant seminarians learned—that Moses had not written the first five books of the Old Testament; that none of the four Gospels were written by the individuals whose names they bear, and that none had been written by an eyewitness to the life of Jesus; and that the Old Testament prophecies believed to foretell the coming of Jesus did no such thing but were rather the fruit of elaborate efforts by the gospels' authors to construct a prophetic prediction of the Messiah out of whole cloth. The dates at which the various books of the Bible had actually been written had been discovered; the often painfully political process by which certain books were ushered into the canon while others were consigned to apocryphal obscurity had been made clear. Scholars untangled the three distinct Hebrew traditions that inform the book of Genesis. They revealed the sequence in which the gospels had been written, the degree to which the authors of Matthew and Luke had drawn on the gospel attributed to Mark, and the necessity for there to have existed another source document, now lost, from which Matthew and Luke borrowed shared elements not taken from Mark. They determined which letters of Paul were authentic (and hence the oldest Christian scriptures, as they predated the gospels) and which were later forgeries composed to achieve specific pastoral agendas. Such were the fruits of almost two centuries of what was sometimes called the Higher Criticism.

Yet the most important—and potentially subversive—discovery to emerge from this Niagara of scholarship was the realization that Jesus, if he even existed, had said and done only a fraction of the things the gospels claimed he had said and done; what is more, the trope of his resurrection from the dead is almost surely mythic. Scholars from Hermann Samuel Reimarus to David Strauss to, eventually, Albert Schweitzer strove to pull aside the veils of legend and shed light on the "actual" historic Jesus.

By the time Schweitzer published his *The Quest of the Historical Jesus* in 1906 (first English translation, 1910), the Higher Criticism had largely spent its momentum. But no matter; Protestant ministers (and eventually, Catholic priests as well) emerged from their seminaries understanding their creeds far differently than did their congregants in their pews. There was much fear (probably justified) that if rank-and-file believers learned what their pastors knew, great numbers would lose their faith. So most of the world's Christian clergy embarked on a strategy of silence. For generation after generation, clergy graduated from seminary knowing that much of what their flocks believed was the stuff of children's storybooks, but they said nothing about it from the pulpit. The rich deposit of the Higher Criticism lay out of reach of the lay faithful, mustering in daunting scholarly tomes (many of which, as an added bonus, were in German). So for decades, the cover-up of what almost two centuries of scholarship had revealed about Christian origins— a cover-up that required the complicity of almost every mainstream to liberal cleric—was astonishingly successful. By the mid-twentieth century, a few popularizing works and muckraking bestsellers had suggested to lay audiences what knowledge lay hidden, but still, too much remained in the shadows.

It was this secrecy that the Religion and Biblical Criticism Research Project hoped to pierce. In short order, it became apparent that even that ambitious agenda was too narrow. Scholars and scientists had powerful new tools at their disposal, to say nothing of a cornucopia of twentieth-century archaeological findings. Could the hunt for Christianity's origins—and especially the quest for the historical Jesus, which had gone largely dormant after Schweitzer—be rekindled?

The Council held what would become the best-attended conference in its history at the University of Michigan at Ann Arbor in April 1985. The eight hundred persons who thronged the "Jesus in History and Myth" conference included a remarkable cross section of the world's religion scholars. The conference apparently reawakened scholarly interest in historical-Jesus studies. In a development for which the Council can claim only the most incidental credit, biblical scholar Robert W. Funk (1926–2005), who had reportedly attended the Ann Arbor event, shortly afterward founded the independent Jesus Seminar. Under the auspices of the Jesus Seminar, about 150 critical scholars gathered over the next two decades, controversially voting by dropping colored beads into jars to decide, among other things, that only about twenty percent of the sayings the gospels attribute to Jesus of Nazareth were authentic. Traditionalists were outraged; more radical theologians regretted that the Jesus Seminar played it so safe, for example, taking the existence of an actual historic Jesus largely for granted.

The Ann Arbor conference also had important internal consequences for the Council and its religion-scholarship efforts.

There, the Council's Academy of Humanism (now the International Academy of Humanism) announced the formation of the Committee for the Scientific Examination of Religion (CSER, pronounced *Caesar*). CSER's brief was nothing less than "to submit religious claims to careful scientific and scholarly investigation and analysis" (*FI*, Summer 1985). Once again, "scientific" was meant broadly, creating the interdisciplinary blend of the hard sciences with history, linguistics, and related fields that ever since has been a hallmark of this effort.

Over the years, CSER has known times of feast and famine. At its high points, it has held important conferences and spawned significant books, sometimes providing a gathering place for scholars who found the headline-grabbing Jesus Seminar too orthodox. Its members made noteworthy contribution to the scholarly discourse surrounding the 9/11 attacks (see Ibn Warraq's "Virgins? What Virgins?") and the controversy over the publication of Danish cartoons lampooning the "prophet" Muhammad (see R. Joseph Hoffmann's "Mutt, Jeff, and Muhammad"). I'm proud to say that *Free Inquiry* was the first major U.S. periodical to reprint a selection of the cartoons (April/May 2006), following several months in which American media editorialized widely about the images without trusting their readers to see for themselves what all the shouting was about. The Borders bookstore chain—and in Canada, the commonly owned Chapters, Indigo, and Coles chains—barred *FI* from its shelves, only to be compelled by public outcry to put it back. (This was an early demonstration of the power of the blogosphere to shape public opinion and pressure corporate actors with unprecedented rapidity.) So we might say that the scientific examination of religion has led us to strange consequences, some of them far removed from the staid domains of the laboratory or the classroom.

Each article in this volume is presented as it originally appeared, and should thus be viewed as a product of its time. The reader should be aware that facts may have changed since an item was originally published. In particular, the capsule biographies of the authors are presented as they appeared at the time of original publication. Not a few authors may have moved to a different institution, published additional books, retired, or died since their articles saw print; not a few more may do the same between the time this book is printed and the time you read it. Hence our decision to present authors' bios as they accompanied their published work.

Appropriately, a panoply of disciplines is represented in this volume. Michael Martin, Tom Shipka, and Ronald A. Lindsay hail from the domain of philosophy; Robert M. Price, Ibn Warraq, Gerd Lüdemann, R. Joseph Hoffman, Laura Purdy, and David Trobisch represent various streams of the broad field of religious studies. Richard Dawkins is a biologist, though his contribution here lies closer to philosophy. Taner Edis is a physicist, though his essay in these pages partakes more of religious history. Victor Stenger applies his discipline (physics, once again) to thorny issues in theology. And Philip Appleman draws on all the sciences—indeed, on the full smorgasbord of human knowledge—to compose the soaring, lyrical essay that brings this volume to a close.

It is also worth noting that David Trobisch's article "Who Wrote the New Testament?," based on a paper delivered at a memorable CSER conference at the University of California at Davis, won the Selma V. Forkosch Award for the best article published in *Free Inquiry* during the year 2007.

Herewith, *The Scientific Examination of Religion*.

THREE NEW ARGUMENTS FOR NONBELIEF

Michael Martin

In this essay, I will present three fresh arguments to justify non-belief in the theistic God usually associated with Christianity and Judaism. First, the Argument from Incoherence shows that the concept of God is like the concept of a round square or a four-sided triangle. Round squares or four-sided triangles cannot exist; neither can God. Second, the Argument from Non-belief was originally presented by contemporary American philosopher Theodore Drange. Especially relevant to evangelical Christianity and Orthodox Judaism, it maintains that the large amount of nonbelief in the world makes the existence of God improbable. Third is a new Moral Argument for Nonbelief constructed by contemporary Canadian philosopher Raymond Bradley. It turns on the conflict between the view that God would not cause or condone immoral acts and biblical statements in which God does precisely this.

These three arguments are relatively new. Though versions of the Argument from Incoherence are centuries old, the version I present here combines various insights developed mainly over the last twenty-five years. Drange put forth his Argument from Nonbelief in 1998, and Bradley's version of the Moral Argument was published in 2000.

It should be noted that theism can be viewed from both a philosophical perspective and a biblical standpoint. According to the philosophical perspective, God is an all-knowing (omniscient), all-powerful (omnipotent), all-good (omnibenevolent) disembodied being who created the Universe. This view is rather abstract and remote, compared with the more popular concrete concept of God held by ordinary men and women and assumed in the Bible. On the biblical view, God is personal: He can be understood by analogy to a human person, and human beings can enter into a personal relation with Him, petitioning Him in prayer and referring to Him as "Thou."

Let us call the first view the God of the philosophers, and the second view the God of the Bible. In what follows I will touch on both.

THE ARGUMENT FROM INCOHERENCE

One good reason not to believe that God exists is that the very concept of God is incoherent, in the same way as is the concept of a round square or the "largest number." In accordance with our two perspectives, philosophical and biblical, this argument can be made in two ways:

First, some properties attributed to God in the Bible are inconsistent.[1] For example, God is said to be invisible (Col. 1:15, 1 Tim. 1:17, 6:16), a being that has never been seen (John 1:18, 1 John 4:12). Yet several people in the Bible, among them Moses (Exod. 33:11, 23), Abraham, Isaac, and Jacob (Gen. 12:7, 26:2; Exod. 6:3) report having seen God. God is supposed to have said, "You cannot see my face, for no one can see me and live" (Gen. 32:30). However, Jacob saw God and lived (Gen. 32:30). In some places God is described as merciful[2], in others as lacking mercy[3]; in some places as a being who repents and changes His mind[4], in others as a being who never repents and changes His mind[5]; in some places as a being who deceives and causes confusion and evil[6], and in others as a being who never does[7]; in some places as someone who punishes children for their parents' wrongdoing[8], and in others as one who never does.[9] So if one takes what the Bible says seriously, God cannot exist.

The Argument from Incoherence can also be made by showing that the attributes specified in philosophical accounts of God are either in conflict with one another, or are internally inconsistent. In my book *Atheism: A Philosophical Justification,* I spend thirty pages analyzing in detail the incoherence connected with the concepts of omniscience, omnipotence, and divine freedom. Here, I only have space to outline the case regarding omniscience.

1. In one important sense, to say that God is omniscient is to say that God is all-knowing. To say that God is all-knowing entails that He has all knowledge that there is. Now philosophers have usually distinguished three different kinds of knowledge: *propositional, procedural,* and *knowledge by acquaintance.* Propositional knowledge is factual knowledge, the knowledge that something is the case. Procedural knowledge, or knowledge how, is a type of skill, and is not reducible to propositional knowledge.[10] Finally *knowledge by acquaintance* is direct experience with some object, person, or phenomenon.[11] For example, to say "I know Mr. Jones" implies that one has not only detailed propositional knowledge about Mr. Jones, but direct acquaintance with him. Similarly, to say "I know poverty" implies that, beside detailed propositional knowledge of poverty, one has some direct experience of it.

To say that God is all-knowing, then, is to say that God has all propositional knowledge, all procedural knowledge, *and* all knowledge by acquaintance. This has implications for the existence of God that usually have not been noticed. First, God's omniscience conflicts with His disembodiedness. If God were omniscient, then God would have all knowledge, including, for example, knowledge of how to swim. Yet only a being with a body can have such procedural knowledge—that is, actually possess the *skill* of swimming—and by definition God does not have a body. Therefore, God's attribute of being disembodied and His attribute of being omniscient are in conflict. Thus, if God is both omniscient and disembodied, God does not exist. Since God is both omniscient and disembodied, therefore He does not exist.

The property of being all-knowing also conflicts with certain moral attributes usually attributed to God. If God is omniscient, He has knowledge by acquaintance of all aspects of lust and envy. But one aspect of lust and envy is *having feelings* of lust and envy. However, God is typically conceived as being morally perfect, and His being morally perfect excludes these feelings. Consequently, there is a contradiction in the concept of God. Consequently, God does not exist.[12]

In addition, God's omniscience conflicts with His omnipotence. Since God is omnipotent He cannot experience fear, frustration, and despair.[13] For, in order to have these experiences, one must believe that one is limited in power. But since God is all-knowing and all-powerful, He knows that He is not limited in power. Consequently, He cannot have complete knowledge *by acquaintance* of all aspects of fear, frustration, and despair. On the other hand, since God is omniscient He *must* have this knowledge. So if one takes philosophical accounts of God seriously, God cannot exist.[14]

THE ARGUMENT FROM NONBELIEF

A second reason for disbelieving in God is the large number of nonbelievers in the world.[15] The Argument from Nonbelief is especially telling against evangelical Christianity, although it has some force against other religions, for example, Orthodox Judaism. Evangelical Christianity asserts that (1) God is merciful and all-loving, compassionate and caring towards humanity; (2) The Bible, and *only* the Bible, is *the* source of God's word; (3) God wants all humans to be saved; (4) A necessary condition for being saved is becoming aware of the word of God and accepting it.

Supposing for the sake of the argument that evangelical Christianity is true, it is difficult to understand why there are nearly one billion nonbelievers in the world. How can a merciful God, a God who wants all humans to be saved, *not* provide clear and unambiguous information about His word to humans when having this information is necessary for salvation? Yet, as we know, countless millions of people down through history have not been exposed to the teaching of the Bible. Those who have been were often exposed in superficial and cursory ways that were not conducive to acceptance. Even today there are millions of people who, through no fault of their own, either remain ignorant of the Christian message or, because of shortcomings in their religious education, reject it. One would expect that, if God were rational, He would have arranged things in such a way that there would be more believers.

Here are a few obvious ideas about how God could have done this:

1. God could have made the Bible more plausible. He could have made it free from contradictions, factual errors, and false or ambiguous prophecies.

2. God could have provided people with exposure to the Bible's message, say, by putting Bibles in every household in the world in the occupants' native language.

3. God could have spoken from the heavens in all known languages so that no human could doubt His existence and His message.

4. God could have sent angels disguised as human preachers to spread His word, empowering them to perform unambiguous miracles and works of wonder.

5. God could have implanted a belief in Himself and His message in every person's mind.

6. In recent times, God could have communicated with millions of people by interrupting prime-time television programs to present His message.

Any and all of these methods, and countless others I have not mentioned, would increase the number of believers and presumably the number of saved people. Yet, God has used none of them.

There are a number of defenses against the Argument for Nonbelief that I should briefly mention:

1. *The Free Will Defense:* Theists might argue that God wants His creatures to believe in Him without coercion. The above suggestions, it might be said, involve *making* people believe in God, and that would interfere with their free will.

However, none of my suggestions about how God could increase people's belief in Him limit free will. For example, to provide people with clear and unambiguous evidence of His existence hardly interferes with free will, since they can reject this evidence. Further, in the Bible God is said to have performed spectacular miracles that influenced people to believe in Him. For example, in Exodus 7:5 God performs a miracle to demonstrate to Israelites that He is the true God. Even if God were to implant belief in Himself in people's minds, they could reject the implanted idea. Moreover, it makes no sense to suppose that a rational God would create human beings in His own image, yet expect them to be so irrational as to believe in Him without strong evidence.

2. *The Testing Defense:* Some evangelical Christians rebut the Argument from Nonbelief by saying that the evidence for God is clear and unambiguous, but humans have rejected it because of spiritual defects such as false pride. Those who accept the evidence pass the test; those who do not accept it fail the test.

However, there is no reason to suppose that evidence for God is convincing and that people reject it because of some spiritual defect. A more plausible hypothesis is that the evidence for God is utterly unconvincing. In addition, even if it were convincing, billions of people because of their backgrounds or circumstances have not been exposed to it. Moreover, if the Bible is convincing in principle, and humans have been exposed to it, they may not see that it is true because of faulty reasoning. It is grossly unfair to punish people for not believing in God either because they have not been exposed to His teachings, or because of an error of reasoning.

3. *The Unknown Purpose Defense:* Theists might argue that God has some unknown reason for permitting so many nonbelievers to exist. However, God has properties that make His having an unknown purpose for permitting so much nonbelief implausible. Thus, according to evangelical Christianity, God wants humans to love Him. How can He want this, and yet fail to make billions of humans aware of the gospel message, since loving Him presupposes being aware of His message? The appeal to unknown purposes at worst makes God appear irrational, and at best creates a mystery that detracts from the explanatory power of theism.[16]

BRADLEY'S MORAL ARGUMENT (MA)

Bradley presents a moral argument for the nonexistence of God by showing that four basic claims associated with the Bible are in conflict[17]:

1. Any act that God commits, causes, commands, or condones is morally permissible.

2. The Bible reveals to us many of the acts that God commits, causes, commands, or condones.

3. It is morally impermissible for God to commit, cause, command, or condone acts that violate our moral principles.

4. The Bible tells us that God does in fact commit, cause, command, or condone acts that violate our moral principles.

There are great difficulties standing in the way of anyone who wishes to deny any of these claims, yet since they are in conflict, at least one of them *must* be denied. To deny the first claim—that any act of God that commits, commands, and so on is morally permissible—would be to admit that God is immoral or even evil. But this would mean that He is not worthy of worship. To deny the second claim—that the Bible reveals to us many of the acts that God commits, commands, and so on—would be to give up the foundation of religious and moral epistemology. If this claim is false, then how can we know *what* we ought or ought not to do? The Bible, according to theists, is the major source of our knowledge of ethical principles. To deny the third claim—that it is morally impermissible for God to commit, command, and so on acts that violate our moral principle—would mean that it is morally permissible to perform acts such as deliberately slaughtering innocent men, women, and children; making people cannibalize their friends and family; practicing human sacrifice; or torturing people endlessly for their beliefs. It would be to align God with moral monsters such as Hitler, Stalin, and Pol Pot. No theist who believes the Ten Commandments or the Sermon on the Mount could deny that this third claim is true.

This leaves the last claim. But the Bible states clearly that God does indeed commit, cause, command, and condone acts that violate our moral principles. God drowned the whole human race except Noah and his family.[18] He punished King David for carrying out a census that God himself had ordered, and He followed David's request to punish others by sending a plague that killed 70,000 people.[19] He commanded Joshua to kill old and young, little children and women, the inhabitants of some thirty-one kingdoms.[20] God says in many places that He has made or will make people cannibalize their own children, husbands, wives, parents, and friends because they have disobeyed Him. God condones Jephthah's act sacrificing his only child as a burnt offering.[21] Finally, God will torture a large portion of the human race in Hell for not believing in Jesus.[22]

Can this moral argument be challenged? One possible strategy apologists might use is to re-interpret biblical passages such as those I have cited in a way that renders them morally harmless. Another is to try to show that our moral principles do not apply to the situations previously described, or that they allow exceptions that would acquit God for having broken them.

Consider the first strategy. With respect to God's threatening to make people cannibalize their own friends and relatives, apologists have offered two rationalizations. First, they have argued that God does not carry out the threat. Second, they argue that these are simply predictions of what will befall the Israelites at the hands of their enemies. However, there are problems with both replies. If they are threats, since God did not carry them out they are empty; hence, God is unreliable. Moreover, it is hard to see how a good and merciful God can make threats of immoral actions. If they are predictions, then God has said something false. Moreover, in the case of Jeremiah, it is clear that God is not predicting what the Israelites' enemies will do, but what *He* will do.

With respect to the second strategy, it might be argued that there are exceptions to the moral principles against torturing innocent people endlessly, performing child sacrifice, and slaughtering innocent people. For example, it might be suggested that God is exempt from these principles even though they are binding on humans. But this double standard makes God less than holy and not worthy of worship. Another tactic is to invoke the doctrine of original sin, that every human being is born in sin, and argue that God is acting on the overriding principle that sin must be punished. So God has the right to punish us as he sees fit. There are, however, two problems with this reply. One is that the doctrine of original sin is implausible. How can newborn babes be held responsible for an inherited and, in their own cases, unactualized disposition to sin? That point aside, this principle would allow human beings to slaughter anyone they like and justify their actions in terms of the punishment of original sin. If slaughtering newborn babies is morally permissible for God, why not for humans too?

So I see no way out of Bradley's problem for theists. They must give up at least one of the above claims—either that the acts of God are morally permissible, or that the Bible reveals to us what those acts are. If they abandon the first, they give up belief in God's holiness; if they abandon the second, they give up the belief that the Bible is His revelation.

Conclusion

I have presented three arguments here for nonbelief in the theistic God. The Augment from Incoherence provides good reasons for rejecting both the God of the philosophers and the God of the Bible. The Argument from Nonbelief is especially effective against evangelical Christianity and Orthodox Judaism, which base their doctrines mainly on biblical considerations and not on abstract philosophical arguments. The Moral Argument provides good reasons for not believing in the God of the Bible. It goes without saying that these three arguments do not constitute the entire case for nonbelief. On the one hand, there are other strong arguments that I have not examined here (see my *Atheism,* Part 2). On the other, in addition to the many arguments *for* atheism there are devastating arguments *against* theism; or to put it another way, there are refutations of arguments that claim to show that God does exist. Indeed, I know of no argument for God that stands up under critical scrutiny (see my *Atheism,* Part 1). So, given the arguments for atheism and against theism, I think it can safely be said that the case for nonbelief is extremely strong.

Notes

1. I am indebted here to Ted Drange, *Nonbelief and Evil* (Amherst, N.Y.: Prometheus Books, 1998), pp. 80–82.

2. Psalms 86:5, 100:5, 103:8, 106:1, 136:2. 148: 8–9; Joel 2:13; Mic. 7:18; James 5:11.

3. Deut. 7:2, 16, 20:16–17; Josh. 6:21, 10:11, 19, 40, 11:6–20; Isa. 6, 19. 15:3; Nah. 1:2; Jer. 13:14; Matt. 8:12, 13:42, 50, 25:30, 41, 46; Mark 3:29; 2 Thes. 1:8–9; Rev. 14:9–11, 21: 8.

4. Gen. 6:6; Exod. 32:14; 1 Sam. 2:30–31, 15:11, 35; 2 Sam. 24:16; 2 Kings 20: 1–6; Psalms 106:45; Jer. 42:10; Amos 7:3; John 3:10.

5. Num. 23:19; 1 Sam. 15:29; Ezek. 24:14; Mal. 3:6; James 1:17.

6. Gen. 11:7; Judg. 9:23; 1 Sam. 16:14; Lam. 3:38; 1 Kings 22:22–23; Isa. 45:7; Amos 3:6; Jer. 18:11, 20:7; Ezek. 20:25; 2 Thes. 2:11.

7. Deut. 32:4; Psalms 25:8, 100:5, 145:9; 1 Col. 14:33.

8. Gen. 9:22–25; Exod. 20:5, 34:7; Num. 14;18; Deut. 5:9; 2 Sam. 12:14; Isa. 14:21, 65:6–7.

9. Deut. 24:16; 2 Chron. 25:4; Ezek. 18:20.

10. For an account of two types of knowledge—knowing how and knowing that—see Israel Scheffler, *Conditions of Knowledge* (Chicago: Scott, Foresman and Co. 1965).

11. See D.W. Hamlyn, *The Theory of Knowledge* (Garden City, N.Y.: Doubleday, 1970), pp. 104–106.

12. This argument was developed in Michael Martin, "A Disproof of the God of the Common Man," *Question*, 1974, 115–24; Michael Martin, "A Disproof of God's Existence," *Darshana International*, 1970.

13. Cf. David Blumenfeld, "On the Compossibility of the Divine Attributes," *Philosophical Studies*, 34(1978): 91–103.

14. Can my arguments be answered? Of course, one could give a different interpretation of God or of the Old Testament. In so doing one would attempt to show that the concept of God is not incoherent. But any such interpretation must not be arbitrary or otherwise problematic. With respect to conflicting biblical passages, a Christian who read an earlier draft of this essay criticized my method of interpretation as neglecting the central themes and concentrating on what he called "legalistic" details. Unfortunately, he did not venture an opinion about how these details are to be reconciled or how one determines the central themes.

Various objections to my abstract philosophical arguments can, of course, be imagined. One might argue that, since it is not logically possible for God to have all knowledge by acquaintance and all knowledge how, God's knowledge should be limited to factual knowledge. The trouble with this reply, however, is that it would be logically impossible for God to have knowledge that it is logically possible for humans to have. The result is paradoxical, to say the least.

15. See Theodore Drange, *Nonbelief and Evil*. Drange is the first philosopher I know to develop and defend this argument in a systematic way.

16. Although I do not have time to develop this argument with respect to Orthodox Judaism, it is fairly clear how it would proceed. In Orthodox Judaism the question is, Why are there so many descendants of the Israelites who since the time of Moses have rejected one or more of the following: (1) There exists a being who rules the entire universe; (2) This Being has a chosen people, namely, the Israelites; (3) He gave them a set of laws, the Torah, and He wants them and their descendants to follow it? God could have done many things to bring the wayward Israelites back into the fold but He did not.

17. See Raymond D. Bradley, "A Moral Argument for Atheism," *The New Zealand Rationalist and Humanist*, Spring 2000, pp. 2–12.

18. Gen. 7:23.

19. 2 Sam. 24:1–15.

20. Josh. Chapter 10.

21. Judges 11: 10–39.

22. Rev. 13: 8, 14: 10–11.

Michael Martin is emeritus professor of philosophy at Boston University. This article is based on a paper he presented at the Center for Inquiry–International (Amherst, New York).

THE INFANCY GOSPELS

Robert M. Price

NO ACCOUNT IN NAZARETH

The earliest known Gospel, Mark, has no tale to tell of Jesus before his baptism as an adult. There is nothing about a miraculous conception or birth, no angelic annunciation, no child prodigy stories such as we find in the other New Testament Gospels. Considered as an historical figure (which despite all the mythology attaching to him, Jesus may have been), there is nothing at all odd that there should be nothing remarkable about his early, private years. But the more Jesus became a glorified mythic hero in Christian imagination, the more his early life became a puzzle: if Jesus was from the very beginning a god on Earth, what sort of childhood adventures must he have had? Surely the Son of the living God cannot have been merely cooling his heels in Nazareth all that time! The logic is precisely the same as that of Superman, Clark Kent, and Superboy.

I am, as it happens, both a New Testament scholar and a huge comic book fan. Since comic books are the modern American myths, it is not surprising to find parallels between them and ancient myths. And these parallels can be quite helpful for understanding both literatures. In the present case, think of the first version of Superman. He came on the public scene as a superhero for the first time as an adult, in *Action Comics* (1938), having whiled away his early years in Smallville. He took the alias Clark Kent and worked for the *Daily Star* (later the *Daily Planet*), then appeared publicly as Superman. His adventures proved so popular that he got a second title each month, *Superman*. But fans wanted even more, so a new title was added to answer the question many readers were asking: how can Kent keep the secret of his powers all those hours of every day at his desk, taking guff from Perry White and Lois Lane? Worse yet, how could he possibly have passed through childhood and adolescence without blabbing the secret of his super abilities? The answer: he didn't. Already in Smallville, according to the new, revisionist account, mild-mannered Clark Kent had countless adventures as Super*boy*. Eventually, the editors decided to push the whole thing back further, and we began reading the adventures of Super*baby*!

The same sequence occurs in the Jesus legend. From a half-historical story of Jesus as a teacher, healer, and exorcist, the early Christian imagination pushed back Jesus's divinity to his childhood and birth and began filling in the gaps with new stories. (For that matter, as Wilhelm Wrede, Raymond E. Brown, John A. T. Robinson, and others showed, divinity was first attached to the Second Coming, then to the Resurrection, then to the baptism, then to the miraculous birth, and, in John's Gospel, back before creation itself!) There were attempts to answer the question: what was Jesus doing during those "missing" years? And they were filled in, not from any historical memory, but rather from creative inference: what *must* young Jesus have been doing?

THE BABY AND THE BATHWATER

The tales collected into texts like the *Infancy Gospel of Matthew*, the *Gospel of Thomas the Israelite*, the *Arabic Gospel of the Infancy*, and the *Proto-Gospel of James* (variously dating from the second century C.E. on through late antiquity) are one and all theological foreshadowings. Each infers backward from prior beliefs about the adult Jesus Christ. A number have to do with boy Jesus running afoul of scribes and Pharisees, as he does as an adult in the canonical Gospels. In one episode, Joseph takes Jesus to a village scribe, who proposes to teach the lad Torah, starting with the alphabet. Jesus contemptuously tells off the teacher: not only does he know the alphabet, but he also knows the kabbalistic significance of each letter, as the teacher himself does not! For such smart-mouthing, the scribe raps Jesus's knuckles with a ruler—and keels over dead!

In another tale, familiar to the writer(s) of the Koran (sura 5:110–111), young Jesus is modeling clay birds by the stream. Young Pharisees carp that he is violating the Sabbath with such "work," whereupon Jesus claps his hands, bringing the birds to life. Such stories mean to tell us that Jesus's friction with the Jewish authorities goes back to the beginning. It was in the blood and could not have been different.

The young Jesus, a divinity after all, is impatient with foolish mortals. Once a neighborhood kid runs past him and punches him in the arm, whereupon Jesus tells him, "You will go no farther on your way!" And the kid drops dead! Joseph is perturbed and tweaks his son's ear, but he has overstepped his bounds, and Jesus tells him, "It is enough that you should see me, but not touch me! If you knew who I am, you would not grieve me! I am with you now, but I was made before you." But sometimes dad and son got along better. Once Joseph, a carpenter, commissioned to make a bed, has cut one of the beams too short. As he bemoans his error, young Jesus suggests they each take one end of the beam and pull: it stretches to the right length, and Joseph thanks God for such a boy!

The lad Jesus performs various healings. Even his bathwater can heal when taken away and poured on the afflicted. The point? "Jesus Christ: the same yesterday, today, and forever" (Hebrews 13:8). This point becomes even more obvious in one Infancy Gospel story in which Judas Iscariot's mother, hearing of the bathwater cures, brings the infant Iscariot to Jesus for exorcism: already the little creep is showing his true colors by biting everybody he comes near! Sure enough, little Judas tries to take a chunk out of Jesus, but is prevented. Nonetheless, he does manage to hit Jesus a childish blow on the ribcage before the demon leaves him, and guess what? It turns out to be this exact spot where the spear of the Roman guard will pierce his side thirty years hence!

WRITTEN BEFORE THE FOUNDATION OF THE WORLD

All these episodes function the same way prophecies of Jesus did in the early Christian imagination. They believed Jesus's saving deeds had already been predicted by Isaiah, Jeremiah, Hosea, Zechariah, etc. In fact, the Gospel incidents can be shown to be later rewrites of those very same Old Testament passages: no wonder they correspond! The direction of motion is from Jesus backward, not from the prophets forward to Jesus. And even so, originally there were no miracle stories in the early life of Jesus. They were posited later as (fictive) anticipations of what the canonical Gospels have him doing during his public ministry.

This means the whole Gospel story is settled before it happens. Once it unfolds, it will be but a kind of charade, no surprises allowed. The Gospels themselves partake of this kind of narrative structure, which Tzvetan Todorov calls "ritual narrative," where the point is not to entertain the reader by unfolding some plot or mystery initially unknown. Rather the function of such a narrative, revealing its roots in cultic ritual rehearsal (Von Rad's "Theology of Recital") is to rehearse again and again the theological belief underlying the story from start to finish. Monika Hellwig points out the similarity of the baptism and transfiguration stories in the Gospels, in which a heavenly voice proclaims Jesus as God's son (echoed by the human voices of John the Baptist, Simon Peter, Mary of Bethany, and others). She calls such similar scenes "icons"—parallel to one another, different depictions of the same theological point, not different points in historical time. The idea is to celebrate and confess again and again the Christian creed for the sake of which the story is being told. This is why there is no real suspense in the Gospels. The evangelists kill any suspense again and again, on purpose, by telling you from the start that Jesus is going to be betrayed, killed, raised from the dead. Again, no surprises allowed!

Precisely this mode of thought produced the Infancy Gospels and their amusing tales. Their authors mean to present a psychologically grotesque and incredible hero: a Jesus who is God in diapers, never having to learn anything, barely able to contain his irritation with foolish adult mortals. Theirs is a Jesus who cannot have grown emotionally or intellectually: such is the fodder of human biography, not of the tidings of the incarnate Son of God. Protestant theologian Martin Kähler saw this flaw in the "historical Jesus" quest of the nineteenth century. Those scholars sought to distill from the legend-laden Gospels of Matthew, Mark, Luke, and John a human Jesus whose personal and spiritual growth might stand as a model for our own and thus revitalize modern Christianity. Such was the credo of liberal Protestantism. But Kähler objected that such a construct of modern psychology would never produce a Jesus Christ worthy of Christian faith. He would stand on our side of the curtain, not God's, and traditional Christianity would be gone. The ancient and unsophisticated tale-spinners of the Infancy Gospels knew the same thing, so they by no means sought to provide a socio-psycho biography of their savior. Thus the result is more like the legends of Krishna than the life of Gandhi.

MISSING TALES OF MISSING YEARS

Why did these ancient documents drop from sight to such an extent that many modern readers have never heard of them? The real question is, why were they excluded from the canon of the New Testament? My guess is that they were suspected of teaching the heresy of "docetism," the belief that Jesus Christ was not truly human, but only "appeared" (Greek: *dokeo*) to be so, like a myth of Zeus coming down to Earth in human form—or like an angel. Widespread among many Christians, this theology seemed to undermine the doctrine of the physical death of Jesus on the cross, and thus the reality of his saving sacrifice. So it was condemned. Docetism took the Infancy Gospels with it, because anyone can see that the young Jesus they portray is no real human being at all! He knows everything and needs to learn nothing. He is a god trapped in a boy's body.

But didn't I just argue that this depiction of Jesus was consistent with Christian belief in his true divinity, no mere human "religious founder"? Well, yes. But the process of hammering out the dogma of Jesus Christ was a series of pendulum swings between Christologies (theologies of Christ) highlighting his divinity and those accentuating his humanity. The theologians wanted to come down right in the middle, with a Jesus who had been true God and true man, one person with both these natures. But depending where you stood, the middle point looked quite different. It's all in the eye of the believer. And while the tales of the boy God were clearly set against a merely human Jesus, the tables turned easily to show that what they depicted was a merely divine Jesus, and that proved to be equally heretical!

Robert M. Price is professor of biblical criticism at the Center for Inquiry and author of Deconstructing Jesus.

WHO OWNS THE ARGUMENT FROM IMPROBABILITY?

Richard Dawkins

"Life is too improbable to be due to chance" is the old standby, the creaking warhorse relied upon by all creationists, from naïve Bible-jocks who don't know any better to comparatively well-educated intelligent design "theorists" who should. In truth, there *is* no other creationist argument (if you discount absurdities such as "Evolution violates the second law of thermodynamics" and falsehoods such as "There aren't any intermediate fossils").

However superficially different various probability arguments may appear, under the surface their deep structure is always the same. In Fred Hoyle's version, the spontaneous emergence of life is as improbable as a hurricane blowing through a junkyard having the luck to assemble a Boeing 747. Something in nature—an eye, a biochemical pathway, or a cosmic constant—is too improbable to have come about by chance. (So far, the argument is impeccable. Now comes the false step.) Therefore, it must have been designed. A watch demands a watchmaker. As a gratuitous bonus, the watchmaker always turns out to be the Christian god (or Yahweh, or Allah, or Lord Krishna, or whichever deity happened to dominate the speaker's personal childhood).

Not only is it wrong to assume that deliberate design is the *only* alternative to chance: deliberate design is not an alternative to chance at all. The only known alternative to chance as an explanation for living complexity is natural selection. And, to those who understand it,[1] it is a brilliantly successful alternative.

Intelligent design "theory" (ID) has none of the innocent charm of its old-style, revival-tent parent. Sophistry dresses up the venerable watchmaker in two cloaks of ersatz novelty: "irreducible complexity" and "specified complexity." Both are wrongly attributed to recent ID authors, and both arguments are much older. Irreducible complexity, which creationists attribute to Michael Behe, is nothing more than the familiar "What is the use of half an eye?" argument, even if it is now applied at the biochemical or the cellular level. Darwin himself anticipated and demolished the general form of the argument in *The Origin of Species*. For a splendid anthology of replies to it in its biochemical and cellular guise, see "Behe's Empty Box" by John Catalano.[2]

"Specified complexity" takes care of the sensible point that any particular rubbish heap is improbable, with hindsight, in the unique disposition of its parts. A pile of detached watch parts tossed in a box is, with hindsight, as improbable as a fully functioning, genuinely complicated watch. What is special about a watch is that it is improbable in the specified direction of telling the time. Creationists fondly imagine that specified complexity is William Dembski's recent coining. Here is how I expressed it eighteen years ago:

> Complicated things have some quality, specifiable in advance, that is highly unlikely to have been acquired by random chance alone. In the case of living things, the quality that is specified in advance is, in some sense, "proficiency"; either proficiency in a particular ability such as flying, as an aero-engineer might admire it; or proficiency in something more general, such as the ability to stave off death. . . . (*The Blind Watchmaker*, p. 9)

Behe and Dembski correctly pose the problem of specified improbability as something that needs explaining. But the explanation they offer—"intelligent design"—is not even a good candidate solution. It is a lazy cop-out, which is most kindly described as a restatement of the problem. And, worse, it shoots itself in the foot.

First, ID theory is lazy. It poses a problem (statistical improbability) and, having recognized that the problem is difficult, lies down under the difficulty. "I can't see any solution to the problem. Therefore, a Higher Power must have done it." When people write to me, bemused by one or other of the ID books, I invite them to imagine a fictional conversation between the lazy alter egos of two scientists working on a hard problem, say A. L. Hodgkin and A. F. Huxley, who in real life won the Nobel Prize for their brilliant elucidation of the biophysics underlying the nerve impulse.

> "I say, Huxley, this is a terribly difficult problem. I can't see how the nerve impulse works, can you?"
> "No, Hodgkin, I can't, and these differential equations are fiendishly hard to solve. Why don't we just give up and say that the nerve impulse propagates by Nervous Energy?"
> "Excellent idea Huxley, let's write the letter to *Nature* now, it'll only take one line, then we can turn to something easier."

Andrew Huxley's elder brother Julian made a similar point when, long ago, he lampooned Henri Bergson's *élan vital* as tantamount to explaining that a railway engine was propelled by *élan locomotif*. Lamentably, by the way, the only scientist ever to win the Nobel Prize for Literature is Bergson, the arch vitalist.

With the best will in the world, I can see no difference between the laziness of my hypothetical Hodgkin and Huxley and the really lazy luminaries of ID. Yet, so successful is their wedge strategy that they are managing to subvert the schooling of young Americans in state after state, and they are even invited to testify before congressional committees—all this while ignominiously failing to come up with a single research paper worthy of publication in a proper scientific journal.

More important, the argument from improbability, quite apart from being lazy, backfires fatally against the design inference. Conscientiously pursued, the statistical improbability argument leads to a conclusion diametrically opposed to the fond hopes of the creationists. There may be good reasons for believing in a supernatural being (admittedly, I can't think of any), but the argument from improbability is emphatically not one of them. Indeed, the argument from improbability is the most powerful argument I know in favor of atheism and against agnosticism.

The design argument is fatally wounded by infinite regress. The more improbable the specified complexity, the more improbable the god capable of designing it. Darwinism comes through the regress unscathed, indeed triumphant. Improbability, the phenomenon we seek to explain, is more or less defined as that which is difficult to explain. It is obviously self-defeating to try to explain it by invoking a creative being of even greater improbability. Darwinism really does explain complexity in terms of something simpler—which in turn is explained in terms of something simpler still, and so on back to primeval simplicity. It is the gradual, escalatory quality of nonrandom natural selection that arms the Darwinian theory against the menace of infinite regress. I suspect that "inflation theory" may perform a parallel role in cosmology, but I should need to be more learned in theoretical physics before attempting a confident defense of my conjecture. My colleague Daniel Dennett uses the vivid word *crane* for theories that do this kind of explanatory lifting work.

Design is the temporarily correct explanation for some particular manifestations of specified complexity such as a car or a washing machine. It could conceivably turn out, as Francis Crick and Leslie Orgel once facetiously suggested, that evolution was seeded by deliberate design, in the form of bacteria sent from a distant planet in the nose cone of a spaceship. But the alien designers then require their own explanation: ultimately, they must have evolved by gradual and, therefore, explicable degrees. It is easy to believe that the universe houses creatures so far superior to us as to seem like gods. I believe it. But those godlike beings must themselves have been lifted into existence by natural selection or some equivalent crane. The argument from improbability, properly applied, rules out their spontaneous existence *de novo*.

Sooner or later, in order to explain the illusion of design, we are going to have to terminate the regress with something more explanatory than design itself. Design can never be an ultimate explanation. And—here is the point of my title—the more statistically improbable the specified complexity, the more inadequate does the design theory become, while the explanatory work done by the crane of gradualistic natural selection becomes correspondingly more indispensable. So, all those calculations with which creationists love to browbeat their naïve audiences—the mega-astronomical odds against an entity spontaneously coming into existence by chance—turn out to be exercises in eloquently shooting themselves in the foot.

The argument from improbability firmly belongs to the evolutionists. It is our strongest card, and we should instantly turn it against our political opponents (we have no scientific opponents) whenever they try to play it against us. If ever you find yourself arguing with a creationist who tries to hit you with the astronomical improbability of living organization, don't deny the improbability and don't apologize for it. Rejoice in it and go one better, while echoing the *sotto voce* response of Thomas Huxley[3] to Bishop Wilberforce: "The Lord hath delivered him into mine hand." The Argument from Improbability belongs to us, and with a vengeance. God is the ultimate Boeing 747.

Author's Note: This article contains passages from my foreword to Niall Shanks's admirable book *God, the Devil, and Darwin: A Critique of Intelligent Design Theory* (Oxford: Oxford University Press, 2004).

Notes

1. The Nobel Prize-winning French biologist Jacques Monod memorably remarked: "The trouble with natural selection is that everybody thinks he understands it."
2. See www.world-of-dawkins.com/Catalano/box/behe.shtml.
3. Andrew and Julian's grandfather.

Richard Dawkins's most recent book is A Devil's Chaplain: Reflections on Hope, Lies, Science, and Love. *He is the Charles Simonyi Professor of Public Understanding of Science at Oxford University.*

EVERYTHING HAPPENS FOR A REASON

Tom Shipka

I hear the saying "Everything happens for a reason" regularly—sometimes in my philosophy classes, other times in casual conversations, and occasionally in televised interviews. When a speaker drops this line in a conversation, it's as though something that is (a) very profound and (b) obviously true has been proclaimed. Unfortunately, the speaker usually gives no follow-up clarification of what he or she takes this saying to mean, much less any explanation of why it is true. What, then, does "Everything happens for a reason" really mean, and is it true?

If you have an opportunity to interrogate people who say "Everything happens for a reason" about what they mean, you will find that it means different things to different people, and sometimes different things to the same person. Here are some of the more popular interpretations of this saying:

1. *Natural events in the present follow from natural events in the past.* This version is expressed in comments such as "Alexis failed her history exam because she didn't study" or "Ralph has lung cancer due to thirty years of smoking." Had Alexis studied or Ralph abstained from tobacco, the implication is that Alexis would be celebrating her success or Ralph's lungs would be clear.

2. *All events happen by necessity according to a grand plan such that these events could not possibly unfold any differently.* Some attribute this grand plan to a deity as in the statement: "George died yesterday because he had finished all the work on earth that God had assigned to him." This view is theistic determinism, or predestination. Others attribute the grand plan to a nondeistic and inscrutable cosmic force, as in the statement: "George died yesterday because his number was up." This, of course, is fatalism. The implication is that if God or fate had scripted things differently, George would be chugging beer with the boys as he usually does at this hour on his way home from work.

3. *All events, even unfortunate or tragic ones, have a beneficial result that explains or justifies these events.* This version is found in statements such as "Stephanie has stopped drinking since her DUI" or "The South Asian tsunami brought together a divided world in sympathy and compassion for the victims." The implication is that evil is inevitable, but that evil spawns good.

4. *The actual causes of many events are not the apparent causes but surprising and inconspicuous ones.* Thus, a person prone to conspiracy theory might allege that "FDR knew about the Japanese plan to attack Pearl Harbor in 1941, but he chose not to expose it because he wanted the attack to draw America into the war." The implication is that things are not what they seem; dark and dirty secrets lie behind events in the news.

5. *The events that occur in a person's current life are determined by the moral quality of his or her previous life.* A Hindu or Buddhist who believes in karma might observe: "Fred must have done awful things in his last incarnation to suffer so many painful afflictions the past few years." The implication is that a

cosmic justice is at work such that those deserving success or failure, happiness or sorrow, reward or punishment, eventually receive their due.

6. *The causes of some natural events are nonnatural.* This view is expressed in statements such as "AIDS is God's way to punish homosexuals" or "Amy's recovery shows that God answered our prayers." The implications are that there is a transcendent entity that influences or controls the natural realm and that there are ways for humans to solicit or produce intervention by this entity.

Are any of these versions of "Everything happens for a reason" true? Can any be adequately justified by arguments and facts?

Version 1 has strong support in ordinary experience and scientific investigation. The causes of some events are difficult to pin down, however, and the implications of version 1 for human conduct are a subject of great controversy and continuing debate among philosophers and scientists. Are the causes at work in our lives compatible with the freedom that so many of us believe that we have?

Next, it seems clear that three versions cannot be proven and that they rest solely on faith. These include the fatalist rendition of version 2, version 5, and version 6. Version 6 also seems to require one to set aside Ockham's Razor, which suggests that we should always seek the simplest adequate solution or explanation. If a simpler explanation of an event seems quite adequate, why should we pass it by for a more complex one? Also, version 6 must deal with the apparent failure of the great majority of petitionary prayers and the selective nature of God's largesse. Why does God grant the prayers of the Smiths but not those of the Joneses, the Allens, the Stewarts, etc.? Why do some patients leave a hospital on foot and others in a hearse?

Next, the predestination rendition of version 2 requires one to prove the existence of a God that is the direct and immediate cause of all events. Even if success here is possible, which is doubtful if we recall the flurry of criticisms of each of the standard arguments for the existence of God, the fallout is considerable. Human free will is ruled out by such a God, and both good and evil are God's doing. If we take this path, must we next deny the reality of evil to salvage God's reputation?

Version 3 runs into two problems. First, some events seem to trigger few if any beneficial or desirable side effects. Consider the beloved young child whose death drives the mother first to depression and later to suicide or the crack addict who abandons his wife and children, wrecks his career, and turns to crime to support his habit until he takes his own life out of despair and disgust. Not all endings are happy ones.

Second, while it is often possible to find a benefit in even the worst calamities, it is seldom the case that the benefit explains or justifies the calamity. An earthquake destroys a school and kills half or more of the students. This triggers a boom for local funeral directors after a protracted period of relatively few deaths, and the erection of an impressive new school with state-of-the-art technology and smaller classes. Does it make sense to say that these "benefits" justify the deaths of the children? Would one be willing, if one could, to replicate such calamities across the planet for the sake of their beneficial effects in all societies? Only the most morally depraved and cold-hearted among us could possibly answer in the affirmative.

Version 4 has the merit of urging thoroughness and caution in the search for truth. Our explanations of events are sometimes mistaken, as the conviction and imprisonment of innocent persons attest. But version 4 also has liabilities. It can invite excessive skepticism and stubbornness, causing one to look needlessly beyond adequate explanations. When the facts clearly support a hypothesis or conclusion, reasonable people should acknowledge it and move on. Facts should trump biases, hopes, wants, and fears. Dwelling indefinitely on the past in the hope of uncovering some dark, deep secret or confirming a pet theory is a waste of time and a diversion from matters more deserving of our attention.

In a nutshell, if one takes "Everything happens for a reason" to mean anything beyond "Natural events in the present flow from natural events in the past," one makes needless and unproven assumptions (2, 5, 6), puts an overly optimistic spin on the flow of history (3), or risks superfluous and indefinite investigation (4).

Tom Shipka is a professor in and chair of the Department of Philosophy and Religious Studies at Youngstown University.

VIRGINS? WHAT VIRGINS?

Ibn Warraq

After the terrorist attacks on September 11, 2001, Richard Dawkins urged me to take a more active role in public discussions of Islam. He suggested that I submit articles to the London Guardian, *which often published his essays.*

The article below was my second for the Guardian *and appeared on January 12, 2002. It attracted the attention of freelance journalist and author Alexander Stille, who telephoned me several times, and whom I put in touch with the scholars mentioned in my article. These discussions and Stille's further interviews resulted in his front-page article, "Scholars Are Quietly Offering New Theories of the Qur'an" (* The New York Times, *March 2, 2002). The revelation that, according to Christoph Luxenberg's interpretation, there were no virgins but rather raisins awaiting the misguided martyrs, proved irresistible to world media. The story was reprinted around the world, from Beijing to Casablanca, and even formed the basis of a Broadway comedy routine by Robin Williams. It's worth looking back on how the "raisin theory" first came to the attention of the general public.*

In August 2001, the American television network CBS aired an interview with a Hamas activist, Muhammad Abu Wardeh, who

48

recruited terrorists for suicide bombings in Israel. Abu Wardeh was quoted as saying: "I described to [a potential bomber] how God would compensate the martyr for sacrificing his life for his land. If you become a martyr, God will give you seventy virgins, seventy wives, and everlasting happiness." Wardeh was, in fact, shortchanging his recruits, since the reward in Paradise for martyrs is seventy-two virgins. But I am getting ahead of myself.

Since September 11, news stories have repeated the story of suicide bombers and their heavenly rewards, and equally, Muslim scholars and Western apologists of Islam have repeated that suicide is forbidden in Islam. Suicide (*qatlu nafsi-hi*) is not referred to in the Qur'an but is indeed forbidden in the Traditions (*Hadith*, in Arabic), which are the collected sayings and doings attributed to the Prophet, and traced back to him through a series of putatively trustworthy witnesses. They include what was done in his presence that he did not forbid, and even the authoritative sayings and doings of the companions of the Prophet.

But the Hamas spokesman correctly uses the word *martyr* (*shahid*) and not *suicide bomber*, since those who blow themselves up almost daily in Israel and those who died on September 11 were dying in the noblest of all causes, *Jihad*, which is an incumbent religious duty, established in the Qur'an and in the Traditions as a divine institution, and enjoined for the purpose of advancing Islam. While suicide is forbidden, martyrdom is everywhere praised, welcomed, and urged: "By the Being in Whose Hand is my life, I love that I should be killed in the way of Allah; then I should be brought back to life and be killed again in His way. . . "; "The Prophet said, 'Nobody who enters Paradise will ever like to return to this world even if he were offered everything except the martyr who will desire to return to this world and be killed ten times for the sake of the great honor that has been bestowed upon him'" (Sahih Muslim, *The Merit of Jihad and the Merit of Martyrdom*, Chapters 781 and 782).

What of the rewards in Paradise? The Islamic Paradise is described in great, sensual detail in the Qur'an and the Traditions; for instance, sura 56, verses 12–40; sura 55, verses 54–56; sura 76, verses 12–22. I shall quote the celebrated Penguin translation by N. J. Dawood of sura 56, verses 12–39: "They shall recline on jewelled couches face to face, and there shall wait on them immortal youths with bowls and ewers and a cup of purest wine (that will neither pain their heads nor take away their reason); with fruits of their own choice and flesh of fowls that they relish. And theirs shall be the dark-eyed *houris*, chaste as hidden pearls: a guerdon for their deeds. . . . We created the *houris* and made them virgins, loving companions for those on the right hand. . . ."

One should note that most translations, even those by Muslims themselves, such as A. Yusuf Ali and the British Muslim, Marmaduke Pickthall, translate the Arabic word *Abkarun* as "virgins," as do well-known lexicons, such as the one by John Penrice. I emphasize this fact, since many prudish and embarrassed Muslims claim that there has been a mistranslation, that *virgins* should be replaced by *angels*. In sura 55, verses 72–74, N. J. Dawood translates the Arabic word *hur* as "virgins"; the context makes it clear that "virgin" is the appropriate translation: "Dark-eyed virgins sheltered in their tents (which of your Lord's blessings would you deny?) *whom neither man nor jinnee will have touched before*" [emphasis added]. The word *hur* occurs four times in the Qur'an and is usually translated as a "maiden with dark-eyes."

There are two points that need to be noted. First, there is no mention anywhere in the Qur'an of the actual number of virgins available in Paradise, and second, the dark-eyed damsels are available for all Muslims, not just martyrs. It is once again in the Islamic Traditions that we find that the seventy-two virgins in heaven are specified: in a *Hadith* (Islamic tradition) collected by Al-Tirmidhi (died 892 C.E.) in the *Book of Sunan* (volume 4, chapters on "The Features of Paradise as described by the Messenger of Allah [Prophet Muhammad]," Chapter 21: "About the Smallest Reward for the People of Paradise," *Hadith* 2687). The same *Hadith* is also quoted by Ibn Kathir (died 1373 C.E.) in his Qur'anic commentary (*Tafsir*) of Sura Al-Rahman (55), verse 72: "(the Prophet Muhammad was heard saying): 'The smallest reward for the people of Paradise is an abode where there are 80,000 servants and seventy-two wives, over which stands a dome decorated with pearls, aquamarine, and ruby, as wide as the distance from Al-Jabiyyah [a Damascus suburb] to Sana'a [Yemen].'"

Modern apologists of Islam try to downplay the evident materialism and sexual implications of such descriptions, but as the *Encyclopaedia of Islam* says, even orthodox Muslim theologians such as al Ghazali (died 1111 C.E.) and Al-Ash'ari (died 935 C.E.) have "admitted sensual pleasures into Paradise." The sensual pleasures are graphically elaborated by Al-Suyuti (died 1505 C.E.), Qur'anic commentator and polymath. He wrote:

> Each time we sleep with a *houri* we find her virgin. Besides, the penis of the Elected never softens. The erection is eternal; The sensation that you feel each time you make love is utterly delicious and out of this world and were you to experience it in this world you would faint. Each chosen one [i.e., Muslim] will marry seventy [*sic*] *houris*, besides the women he married on earth, and all will have appetizing vaginas.

One of the reasons Nietzsche hated Christianity was that it

"made something unclean out of sexuality," whereas Islam, many would argue, is sex-positive. One cannot imagine any of the Church fathers writing ecstatically of heavenly sex as Al-Suyuti did, with the possible exception of St. Augustine before his conversion! But surely, to call Islam sex-positive is to insult all Muslim women, for sex is seen entirely from the male point of view; women's sexuality is admitted but seen as something to be feared, repressed, and a work of the devil.

Scholars have long pointed out that these images are clearly drawn pictures and must have been inspired by the art of painting. Muhammad, or whoever is responsible for the descriptions, may well have seen Christian miniatures or mosaics representing the gardens of Paradise and has interpreted the figures of angels rather literally as those of young men and young women. A further textual influence on the imagery found in the Qur'an is the work of Ephrem the Syrian (306–373 C.E.), *Hymns on Paradise*, written in Syriac, an Aramaic dialect and the language of Eastern Christianity, and a Semitic language closely related to Hebrew and Arabic. This naturally leads to the most fascinating book ever written on the language of the Qur'an, and, if proved to be correct in its main thesis, probably the most important book ever written on the Qur'an. Christoph Luxenberg's book, *Die syro-aramaische lesart des Qur'an* (Berlin: Das Arabische Buch, 2000), available only in German, came out just over a year ago, but has already had an enthusiastic reception, particularly among those scholars with a knowledge of several Semitic languages, at Princeton, Yale, Berlin, Potsdam, Erlangen, Aix-en-Provence, and the Oriental Institute in Beirut.

Luxenberg tries to show that many of the obscurities of the Qur'an disappear if we read certain words as being Syriac and not Arabic. I cannot go into the technical details of his methodology but it allows Luxenberg, to the probable horror of all Muslim males dreaming of sexual bliss in the Muslim hereafter, to conjure away the wide-eyed *houris* promised to the faithful in sura 154, verse 54; sura 52, verse 20, sura 55, verse 72; and sura 56, verse 22. Luxenberg's new analysis, leaning on the Hymns of Ephrem the Syrian, yields "white raisins" of "crystal clarity" rather than doe-eyed and ever-willing virgins—the *houris*. Luxenberg claims that the context makes it clear that it is food and drink that is being offered, and not unsullied maidens or *houris*. In Syriac, the word *hur* is a feminine plural adjective meaning "white" with the word *raisin* understood implicitly. Similarly, the immortal, pearl-like *ephebes* or youths of suras such as sura 76, verse 19 are really a misreading of a Syriac expression meaning "chilled raisins (or drinks)" that the Just will have the pleasure of tasting in contrast to the "boiling drinks" promised to the unfaithful and damned.

As Luxenberg's work has only recently been published, we must await its scholarly assessment before we can pass any judgements. But if Luxenberg's analysis is correct, then suicide bombers, or rather prospective martyrs, would do well to abandon their culture of death, and instead concentrate on getting laid seventy-two times in this world, unless, of course, they would really prefer chilled or white raisins, according to their taste, in the next.

Note: The above article owes much to Y. Feldner's article, "'Seventy-two Black Eyed Virgins': A Muslim Debate on the Rewards of Martyrs," published in MEMRI, October 30, 2001.

Ibn Warraq is a leading critic of Islam and a fellow of the Center for Inquiry. His new book is Leaving Islam: Apostates Speak Out *(Prometheus Books, 2005).*

THE INTOLERANT GOSPEL

Gerd Lüdemann

The Early Christian message announces that God has brought to pass a new epoch. It began with the coming of his son into this world, culminated provisionally in the latter's resurrection from the dead, and was supposed to reach its fulfillment in his imminent Second Coming. The Gospel—its literal translation is "Good News"—has Jesus Christ as its center. The salvation or eternal damnation of individual human beings depends on whether they believe or do not believe in him. "Whoever believes and is baptized will be saved. But whoever does not believe will be condemned"—this is the clear message of the risen Jesus at the end of Mark's Gospel, the first of the four canonical accounts to be written.

But soon, the Good News developed into Threatening News—that is, if the offer of salvation was turned down! Church leaders soon equated right belief with obedience. They projected onto the screen of heaven a social fabric based on subordination and increasingly shaped by a culture of suppression. The canonical status of the New Testament writings—henceforth an eternal norm for the church—has radically blurred the vision of its followers, inhibiting their ability to recognize that all these texts emerged from controversies whose marks they still show.

The Christian church benefited from the destruction of Jerusalem by the Romans in 70 C.E., and until the end of the first century it spread rapidly within the Roman Empire. Indeed, so rapid was its continued growth that a little more than two and a half centuries later this new and formerly outlawed faith became the official religion of the empire. Judaism laid the groundwork for Christianity's enormous success by endowing the church with the high ethical standards of the Old Testament. What an irony of history that the Christian religion showed so little gratitude to her Jewish mother as to relegate her along with other "enemies" of the Gospel to the realm of darkness. Yet in so doing, she did no more than certify her inheritance, for the legacy of Israel included the doctrine of election and with it the exclusive monotheism that judged all other kinds of worship as service to idols.

As an integral part of their missionary efforts, these enthusiastic Christians introduced First Commandment intolerance ("I am Yahweh, your God, you shall have no other gods besides me") into the Greco-Roman world. Oddly enough, it was their own religious tolerance and inclusiveness that afforded the competing Hellenistic religions little chance of asserting themselves against the Christians. Acquiescence, far from being an antidote against the Christian claim of exclusive revelation, allowed the church to take advantage of Rome's laissez-faire politics in religious matters and thus to expand relentlessly.

In this context, it is worth noting that the generally exaggerated accounts of Roman persecutions of Christians were limited in scope and severity. Lusting after martyrdom, many Christians in effect condemned themselves, and many a Roman governor failed to do them the favor of execution. And once they had begun participating in the political power structure, Christian bishops guided the governmental sword against pagans, heretics, and Jews to an extent that far exceeded the intensity of previous persecutions against their coreligionists. This intolerance remained in force until modern times.

Contrary to the popular thesis that Luther's understanding of freedom included tolerance, there can be no doubt about the great reformer's intolerance toward Catholics, Jews, Turks, Gentiles, and Protestant heretics. Rather, humanists and Christian minorities first raised the call for tolerance. And despite the initial lack of success these groups achieved, they finally succeeded against the will of both the Roman and Reformed churches. To be sure, the church's resistance *against* tolerance was, historically speaking, a necessity. For the overall thrust of Holy Scripture, both the Old and New Testaments, is to promote God and his reign and to silence all dissenting voices.

And while "peace" is a central theme in Holy Scripture, the aggressive side of Christian faith is all but certainly responsible for the many bloody wars started in and from Christian Europe. A key issue, of course, is how that peace is to be achieved. Here, the New Testament message is as crystal-clear as it is—at least by modern standards—indefensible: Jesus Christ himself will return to carry out God's will and by force, empowered by the authority of his resurrection, will establish his father's kingdom of peace on earth. On the basis of this promise, believers in Jesus Christ have at all times claimed access to that power and used it with a good conscience against those they perceive to be enemies of the Gospel.

Indeed, intolerance seems to be an inherent, even necessary ingredient of the Christian religion. The noted theologian Karl Barth says it quite openly:

> No sentence is more dangerous or revolutionary than that God is One and there is no other like Him. Let this sentence be uttered in

such a way that it is heard and grasped, and at once 450 prophets of Baal are always in fear of their lives. There is no more room now for what the recent past called toleration. Beside God there are only his creatures or false gods, and beside faith in him there are religions only as religions of superstition, error, and finally irreligion.

Clearly, it would be misleading to think that freedom in general and freedom of religion specifically are the consequence of the Christian message. Indeed, the religious tradition that claims as its founder the Prince of Peace has through the centuries shown an inability to endure other religious viewpoints. And this is as true today as ever, despite the protestations of church leaders who would like to have it appear otherwise in order to retain their welcome within the institutions of power that comprise the secular state.

In reality, neither Christian theology nor the church can champion freedom of religion without betraying a considerable degree of hypocrisy. For tolerance requires an unconditional acknowledgment of the freedom and dignity of human beings without recourse to God. Yet the jealous Yahweh of the Bible, who demands unconditional obedience, can never approve of such liberal affirmations.

Acknowledgments

This essay was first published in German under the title "Intolerantes Evangelium" in *Die Welt am Sonntag*, December 5, 2004. Gerd Lüdemann thanks Tom Hall for editorial work and *Die Welt am Sonntag* for allowing its publication in English. It is a preview of his new book, *Intolerance and the Gospel: Selected Texts from the New Testament* (Prometheus, forthcoming).

Gerd Lüdemann is Professor of History and Literature of Early Christianity at the University of Göttingen, Germany, and the director of the Institute of Early Christian Studies. The university has placed restrictions on his teaching due to his work in religious criticism.

MUTT, JEFF, AND MUHAMMAD

R. Joseph Hoffmann

While the U.S. State Department—hoping to win friends in Iraq for the "American way"—deplores the impropriety in the Danish "Cartoon Crisis," it seems to take in stride, or in ignorance, the continuing anti-Semitic propaganda of Islamic organizations like Hezbollah in Lebanon, which fuels hatred of Israel through the broadcast of television programs such as *Al-Shatat* (*The Diaspora*). That series was bankrolled by Syria and broadcast in Lebanon in 2003 during the month of Ramadan, when Arab TV viewing peaks. It has been in reruns throughout the Middle East ever since.

Al-Shatat consists of twenty-nine episodes—presented daily, soap-opera style—which give a pseudo-history of the Zionist movement from its beginnings in the nineteenth century to the establishment of the State of Israel. The "information" it provides is distorted, false, and rife with anti-Jewish propaganda, caricature, and religious insult. The series, conceived in the spirit of *The Protocols of the Elders of Zion,* focused on the ancient blood libel that the Jews use the blood of Christian children to make Passover *matzoh* (traditional Jewish unleavened bread) and on the "Jewish plot to take over the world." Pathetically enough, its melodramatic subtext was designed to curry favor in the "Christian West"—against the Jews. No one bothered to tell the producers how little secular Europe and distracted America cares about anti-Jewish libel—a blind spot, in terms of historical reality fixes that also explains Muslim incomprehension over Danish (and broader EU) blasphemy.

The reaction of the United States to this incitement? None at all. For the Jews, it was more of the same. No buildings were burned; no mullahs were killed. And the lesson: it is OK to pillory Jews and Christians, a tradition of polemic, caricature, and bitter satire that extends back into late antiquity, and by assimilation supports a habit of self-mockery and irony that makes Jewish (and maybe a few Catholic) comedians funnier than Evangelicals or Muslims. Perhaps the defining characteristic of any religious fundamentalism is its inability to laugh at a joke made at its own expense—as in, "Hal Lindsey, Osama bin Laden, and Baruch Goldstein walk into a bar. The bartender asks, 'Is this some kind of joke?'"

Forget clichés about the "Culture Wars," "intolerance," "the other," "Crusader logic," and "Postcolonial Fatigue Syndrome." Social critic Ibn Warraq is correct in his recent commentary on the "Cartoon Crisis" that the modern West is the Mother of Reason and that no one in Denmark or France needs to be lectured on the value of tolerance. But he's wrong to think that Muslims care a fig about Reason that leaves Paradise behind. They're not reading Hume: they're reading the Muslim philosopher-theologian Al-Ghazali (1058–1111 C.E.), who decreed that it is a sacred duty to "suppress the enemies of religion through the *jihad* in His cause, and to gain their wealth, women, and lands until they surrender to Islam." (Indeed, one of the most amusing of the cartoons shows a worried, diminutive Prophet welcoming smoking suicide bombers with the caption, "Stop,

stop—we ran out of virgins.") The tricky part of tolerance is that those who invoke it as victims hate it in principle.

The West may have an imperfect understanding of Islam; it does not have a completely false understanding of Islam. And the Great Lie that Western governments, especially the perennially incompetent Washington, urge along as it slouches toward Mecca to be born is that "understanding" and freedom of expression—even if it involves torching embassies and killing priests—is the solution to the history of the very incompetence that has led to the crisis.

It is time for the West to live and embrace the secularism it espouses, not to hide behind an outworn creed, a pagan pretense of religious magnanimity, a nutty and defeasible belief that religion is benign and thus should be protected. Expression—instantiated as murder, arson, and riot—proves that some religious views are toxic and cannot be tolerated. To be blunt, the same violent religious "expression" expressed by Jews or Christians domestically would land them in jail, not get them a slot on *Oprah* or a conversation with Bill Moyers.

Do we really do Muslims a favor by forgiving the trespasses we have brought into being through a century and a half of double dealing and political hypocrisy? Do we really want one rule book for secularized Christians and Jews (the vast majority), another for noisy, politically hyperactive, born-again Christians, and a third for noisy and lethal Muslims?

With regard to Islam, Europe and America have not educated or straight-talked; they have domineered, exploited, humiliated, colonized, expropriated, connived, and condescended to the Middle East, winking as the family Saud supplied their needs. They thought the whole world went to the moon in 1969—when the mullahs denied (and many believed them) that anyone had ever been there. It wasn't just a case of the calendar being lunar—a little fact we missed—but a question of whether by setting foot on the moon we had made it Christian. Now we want to know why Muslims fly planes into skyscrapers, bomb weddings in Tel Aviv, and set embassies ablaze in Beirut, when the centerpiece of their religious dignity, their Prophet, is ridiculed, as though he were merely one of them. One thing is certain: they do not do these things because they share with us a definition of peace or a sense of humor.

Quietly, we in the West think that Muslims are crazy, but we dare not say so. Publicly, we say that all religions are created equal, and that the West—really—loves Islam. The name itself comes from the Arabic word for peace, we're told. But it doesn't. It's derived from the word for surrender.

Europe did not create Islam, but it has been preternaturally stupid for centuries in its comprehension of Islamic theology. America may be forgiven, since its preternatural stupidity extends even to Europe. That is why America's desperate effort to curry favor among the Muslim populations of Europe and the Middle East (and at home) by trading free speech for religious tolerance—and oil—betrays its own confusion about the wide religious world that Islam inhabits. Our brightest jurists find themselves playing the role of biblical exegetes in relation to a religious situation Jefferson could not have imagined. Our politicians find themselves perched above a marketplace filled with buyers with funny names and ideas. Our closest allies, the Europeans, whom we privately detest but count on to explain the complexities of things beyond these shores, show us that their pockets are empty of explanations even if their hearts are in the right place.

Who would have guessed that the Prophet's turban, shown in

the most famous cartoon as a bomb with its fuse burning down, would explode in (of all places) Scandinavia?

R. Joseph Hoffmann is the chair of the Committee for the Scientific Examination of Religion and the Religious Studies Department at Wells College.

WHY 'RELIGIOUS LITERACY' IS A MISLEADING CONCEPT

Laura Purdy

"Religious literacy" appears to be a concept whose time has come. For example, the first recommendation of a draft of a major new policy statement, the "Wingspread Declaration on Religion and Public Life" (available at www.svhe.org/files/ WingspreadDeclaration.pdf), emphasizes the urgent need for better education for religious literacy. Yet its content is left uncomfortably vague. The "Wingspread Declaration" calls—perhaps reasonably enough—for students to "learn the relevance of religion to all disciplines." But it also underlines the importance of training teachers to "infuse religion in student learning, without overstepping First Amendment freedoms," without providing any examples of what that might mean.

Moreover, "religious" or "biblical" illiteracy is now clearly seen by many as both a symptom of and a cause of moral decay in the United States. There appear to be at least two different versions of this position. The first is connected with particular religions. For example, John C. Cavadini laments that such ignorance prevents Catholics from becoming "effective agents of moral change." The second appears to be more general, attributing to illiteracy the alleged collapse of morality in society, such that (in the words of one Bible-study guide) "our standards of morality are skewed, where good is evil and evil is good." It is this latter view that I will examine here.

One version of this position is expounded in "Biblical Illiteracy" (a section of the website Bible Study Guides) which recommends daily Bible reading to "increase one's understanding of the Word of God"; preachers "are to give heed to the Word, and to preach the Word . . . providing exposition of the Scriptures . . . not entertaining us with 'pop theology' and 'pop psychology.'" Only in this way are communities allegedly able to adopt and follow moral standards, which include fighting for capital punishment and against abortion, divorce, adultery, fornication, homosexuality, pornography, and promiscuity. More generally, this religious activity will help us stop rewarding "the wicked (movie stars, entertainers) . . . and depriving the good (teachers, etc.)" The implicit message is that the Bible contains moral truths, and we have only to study it to learn and apply them.

Stephen Prothero seems to offer a "lite" version of this position in his influential op-ed piece, "A Nation of Faith and Religious Illiterates," in the *Los Angeles Times* (January 12, 2005). He decries the widespread ignorance of religious texts, rightly attributing to it the confusion in education circles between teaching about religion (constitutional) and promoting religious belief (unconstitutional). He comments, "When Americans debated slavery, almost exclusively on the basis of the Bible, people of all races and classes could follow the debate. They could make sense of its references to the runaway slave in the New Testament book of Philemon and to the year of jubilee, when slaves could be freed. Today it is a rare American who can engage with any sophistication in the biblically inflected arguments about gay marriage, abortion or stem cell research."

What he seems to be suggesting is that such knowledge of

the Bible is a good thing, because it is the basis for communication and common understanding. He also seems to be suggesting (but adroitly manages to avoid asserting) that it is a source (*the* source?) of moral knowledge.

But these are two very different claims. When religion plays a role in moral and political debate, it is crucial for the public to understand both what is said and its context. These days, at the very least, as past Unitarian Universalist Association President John A. Buehrens writes in "Why Liberals Should Read the Bible" (in his book *Understanding the Bible: An Introduction for Skeptics, Seekers, and Religious Liberals*), such knowledge is necessary to provide a different interpretation of fundamentalist claims.

Of course, Buehrens's position *still* supports the suggestion that the Bible can provide concrete moral guidance. And, that is what the very terms *religious* or *biblical literacy* appear to suggest. *Literacy* is now widely used to condemn incompetence in a huge number of areas. A quick Google search turned up related references to the following terms expressed as sorts of literacy: *biblical, constitutional, cultural, ecological, economic, electoral, financial, geographical, health, historical, Internet, investor, mathematical, media, moral, musical, religious, scientific, sexual, statistical,* and *technological.*

But what does *illiteracy* mean, and are all these connected references meaningful? The traditional meaning of the word is quite clear: "inability to meet a certain minimum standard of reading and writing skill" (*Columbia Encyclopedia*, 6th ed.). It also has a much broader meaning, which no doubt informs many of these references: "the condition or quality of being ignorant or unknowledgeable in a particular subject or field" (*American Heritage Dictionary*, 4th ed.). Deciding on a standard and determining whether a given individual meets it is clearly relatively simple in some cases, such as in the ability to read or write. One can also see how this could work in other fields. For example, "financial literacy" might be defined as knowing how to balance a checkbook, understanding how credit cards and interest work, and so forth. But we can begin to see some difficulties already with respect to the related concept of "economic literacy." Some facts, methods, and theories in economics are widely accepted and theoretically well supported, but there is also very fundamental theoretical disagreement about important issues in the field. With respect to the former, it is reasonable to judge that there is knowledge, such that lack of familiarity with it might constitute illiteracy. But with respect to the latter, asserting that the failure to adopt a particular theoretical stance constitutes illiteracy would be a much different affair.

The same would be true for "moral literacy." Philosophers will claim that any such concept must include at least the understanding that both facts and logic are essential for moral judgment, plus familiarity with the various moral theories and their shortcomings and some grasp of metaethics. One would be on much less firm ground claiming that such literacy requires one to adopt any particular theory. But, given the apparently almost universal religious and popular belief that ethics is constituted by the acceptance of principles and rules handed down by some religious authority, it is difficult to escape the conclusion that the concept of moral literacy is essentially contested. Using it, therefore, constitutes an untenable bid to have one's own position accepted without argumentation.

Why then resist the concept of "religious literacy," as defined by those who see it as the key to remedying alleged moral decay—that is, the adoption of moral principles and values they disapprove of? This isn't rocket science, and the issues are widely understood among those educated in the liberal arts. There is no body of ethical truth such that knowing it constitutes knowledge and not knowing it constitutes illiteracy.

The claim that there is such a body of ethical truth arises from erroneous assumptions. One is that ethics is a set of principles and rules handed down by a religious authority. Another is that the only alternative to this position is adoption of a malignant moral relativism that denies the existence of any ethical principles at all. The first objection to this view is that it is fallacious: it is an example of a false dilemma that sees only two options when others exist. In this case, what is ignored is the rich philosophical tradition of ethical and political theory that grounds morality in the conditions of human life.

The second objection was elaborated by Socrates some two thousand years ago against the view that ethics is what the gods command, although it is equally telling against any alleged moral authority. To avoid following arbitrary or wicked judgments, we must make a prior judgment about the authority's moral standing. Existence alone (or, in the case of God, alleged existence) of an authority creates no case for following its commands (except perhaps to escape punishment for failing to do so) and fails to relieve us of the labor of determining for ourselves what is right or wrong. So the idea that spreading this conception of religious literacy will take the United States back to some mythical golden age is simply incoherent. There is no knowledge to provide purchase for such literacy.

What could be said on behalf of "biblical literacy"? It would seem that it would have to include awareness of the best scholarship of the Bible. As Ellis Rivkin notes in *Biblical vs. Secular Ethics: The Conflict* (edited by R. Joseph Hoffmann and Gerald Larue, Prometheus Books, 1988), such scholarship shows that "the Bible was centuries in the making and consists of a diversity of books written at different times for different purposes, by a wide variety of individuals impelled by a wide variety of interests," and, that "sometimes its teachings contradict each other." Thus, the Bible is no "body of agreed upon principles . . . [or] ethics."

It would constitute a huge step forward in helping the public assess the renewed push for a (right-wing) Christian America if that meaning of "religious literacy" were generally accepted. Unfortunately, that is not the case. The term has been preempted by those who promote the idea that accepting their version of allegedly biblically based ethics is the key to recovering a moral society. Humanists should therefore eschew "biblical" or "religious" literacy and seek other language to promote their own views.

Laura Purdy is a professor of philosophy and the Ruth and Albert Koch Professor of Humanities at Wells College. She has authored numerous books and articles on ethics, family issues, and feminism.

A FALSE QUEST FOR A TRUE ISLAM

Taner Edis

We often view Islam as a problem—as the world religion most closely associated with political violence, poverty, and lack of individual freedom. Not only does Islam inspire fervid commitment to revelation, it seems particularly intolerant of critics. Any close observer of Muslim lands can compile a disturbing list of scholars persecuted for nontraditional interpretations of the Qur'an, science educators who have suffered for defending evolution, and even a number of intellectuals assassinated because of their public criticism of Islam.

Secular humanists have, by and large, supported skepticism about Islam. Ibn Warraq regularly writes for *Free Inquiry* urging more attention to Qur'anic criticism. When critics such as Ayaan Hirsi Ali denounce how conservative Muslims treat women, humanists typically agree. And when Salman Rushdie speaks to secularists about the lack of intellectual freedom in Muslim lands, and also castigates Westerners who would give in to censorship due to cultural relativism or fear of violence, he knows he is addressing a sympathetic crowd. Secular humanists care deeply about freedom of inquiry, and they perceive that many threats to this freedom today involve Islam.

Nevertheless, secular humanists have not been entirely clear-eyed about Islam. While supporting critical inquiry, many secularists have also been partial to simplistic representations of the Muslim world. Indeed, some popular secular literature opposing Islam is hardly distinguishable from Christian and neoconservative polemics. Secularists have been too eager to seek immediate doctrinal causes for Muslim problems. In doing so, many critics have been tempted to identify an essential "true Islam" that is antagonistic to reason and liberal values.

Now, there is no denying that Islamic countries are too often intellectual disaster areas. I was born and educated in Turkey and now teach physics at an American university, so I am particularly interested in the Muslim world's troubled relationship with modern science. In my book *An Illusion of Harmony: Science and Religion in Islam* (Prometheus, 2007), I draw the dismal picture of Muslim intellectual life. Muslim scientific productivity is very low. Indeed, if Muslims were to stop contributing to science, the rest of the world's scientific community would hardly notice. Moreover, Muslim cultures are marked by ambivalence about the modern scientific outlook. As a result, Islam harbors some very powerful pseudoscientific beliefs. Large numbers of Muslims from every nationality and sect are convinced that modern scientific and technological developments have been prefigured in the Qur'an. Evolution is almost absent from science education in many Muslim countries; Turkey has produced a very successful creationist movement. Some devout Muslim intellectuals have proposed that physics and biology be centered on divine design and that sociology and history be studied in a revelation-centered manner. Such pseudoscience is espoused by many university professors as well as popular religious leaders. Liberal Muslims would like to reinterpret their religion, but they are much more tentative than their Christian counterparts.

So it is natural to ask whether Islam is incompatible with science. Modern Jews and Christians have, with the exception of fundamentalists, achieved a less conflicted relationship with scientific institutions than their Muslim counterparts. Perhaps there is something specifically about Islam—beyond its commitment to supernatural agents and revealed texts—that impedes scientific thinking.

Many critics of Islam think so. They argue that Islamic doctrines promote distrust of rationality, and they find these doctrines in the sacred texts of Islam or in classical interpretations that continue to define mainstream Islam today. For example, in his 2002 *Islam Unveiled: Disturbing Questions about the World's Fastest-Growing Faith*, Robert Spencer, a well-known anti-Islamic writer, takes the Qur'anic passage 5 Al Maidah 64—"The Jews say the hand of God is bound. *Their* hands are bound, and they are accursed, by what they say . . ."—and interprets it as an objection to Jewish and Christian notions of a created universe that operates according to laws. This, to Spencer, means that Islam does not accept a rational, orderly universe, and hence is antagonistic to science.

But 5 Al Maidah 64 is not about an orderly universe; it is about a long-forgotten dispute with Jews over taking action to prevent immoral acts. Yes, medieval Muslim thinkers emphasized God's complete freedom and omnipotence—to the extent of denying that natural causality had any integrity aside from God's will. They interpreted the Muslim sacred sources accordingly. And, yes, this might have contributed to a religious distrust of secular knowledge. It is a gross misrepresentation, however, to suggest that one medieval interpretation is what naturally proceeds out of the Qur'an and inhibits scientific development. Practically no Muslims today agree with Spencer's reading of the Qur'an.

Perhaps I should set Spencer aside; after all, his attacks on Islam serve a Christian agenda. But many secular critics of Islam, including secularists within the Muslim world, also adopt simplistic views. For example, it is common to blame Muslim intellectual backwardness on al-Ghazali, the great Sunni scholar. About nine hundred years ago, al-Ghazali condemned Greek philosophy and disparaged human reason that did not pursue divine purposes. So mainstream Sunni Islam, the story goes, reflected the influence of al-Ghazali and discouraged science. Indeed, secularists and liberal Muslims often argue that Islam needs to revive rationalist movements such as the Mutazila, which were active in the ninth century. This is also a historically naïve view.

Medieval doctrinal disputes are not productive for understanding the uneasy relationship between science and most varieties of modern Islam. Discussions of al-Ghazali or the Mutazila obscure the very significant discontinuities between modern science and all varieties of medieval thinking. Moreover, emphasizing medieval attitudes that discouraged science and reason ignores how, especially in the last two centuries, most Muslims have been determined to catch up to the West in science and technology. Modern Islamic literature is full of praise of science and reason; indeed, Muslims often insist that Islam is a completely rational religion that encourages scientific inquiry.

Consider the *Nur* movement, which has been deeply involved with all sorts of pseudoscience in Turkey. The movement promotes crude science-in-the-Qur'an fantasies, such as the notion that Qur'anic verses predict modern astrophysics. *Nur* writers draw on parapsychology to defend the reality of a spiritual realm. And the *Nur* movement has been instrumental in developing Islamic creationism, which has recently emerged from

Turkey to become internationally popular. Yet social scientists studying the *Nur* movement remark on how modern-oriented and how science- and technology-positive it is. Indeed, that is an important reason why the *Nur* movement promotes pseudo-science. Anyone trying to explain today's strained relationship between science and Islam has to look at how modern Muslims understand science and their religious tradition—to explore modern religious currents such as the *Nur* movement. The idea that Islam proceeds directly out of sacred texts will only get in the way. Trying to locate an original sin against reason in medieval Islam is, similarly, largely a distraction.

Indeed, attention to Islam as it is actually practiced, rather than focusing on the Qur'an or idealized doctrines of classical Islam, is especially important today. Critics and apologists alike tend to portray Islam as a coherent entity, existing in stagnant (or glorious) continuity with an original revelation and a classical civilization based on that revelation. At the least, this ignores Islam's traumatic encounter with the modern West. In the overcrowded cities of Muslim countries today, Islam appears chaotic, split into many currents that try to assemble different fragments of a religious heritage to create new, modern forms of Islam. Islam is always under construction. We can identify common themes, and, very often, it is legitimate to talk of mainstream Islamic beliefs that contrast with minority points of view. But there is no "true Islam" that can be adequately defined by a list of essential characteristics. Muslim religious scholars often try to speak for true Islam, usually to denounce a rival interpretation that also claims to represent true Islam. Occasionally, scholars reach consensus about who is the heretic. But modernization has also undermined traditional structures of religious authority. An engineer who lacks classical religious training can feel free to lead an urban discussion group mining the sacred sources for contemporary guidance. True Islam is more pious hope than reality.

So, where science is concerned, there is no single Islam to discuss—just a complicated landscape of sometimes rather new religious orientations. The interesting questions concern the continuing cultural weakness of science in conditions of rapid religious change. There is nothing essential to Islam that prevents a more liberal accommodation with science. Religions can change, and how they change depends more on historical contingencies and constraints than on doctrinal essences. The prospects for an improved relationship between popular varieties of Islam and modern science remain bleak, nonetheless.

Much of what I say concerning science also applies to criticism of Islam, in general. Too often, we go on a quest for a true Islam. For example, Qur'an translations sell very well these days, often because Westerners decide to investigate Islam by consulting the holiest text of Muslims. I expect this often produces bewilderment. The Qur'an can be a very disorganized, often opaque text. And, without the context provided by at least a basic acquaintance with Muslim religious culture, just reading the Qur'an is almost no help in understanding Islam. Trying to get the measure of Islam by sitting down with the Qur'an is a mistake—especially if done with the idea that the Qur'an is the key to the true Islam that most Muslims acknowledge.

Unfortunately, some recent secular critics of Islam make just this mistake. The most egregious example has to be Sam Harris, who, in his 2004 *The End of Faith*, portrays Islam as a violence-obsessed religion. He makes his case by presenting a few pages listing verses of the Qur'an that promise sadistic punishments for unbelievers in the afterlife, urge fighting against infidels, and otherwise show an unhealthy preoccupation with vengeance and violence. Harris assumes that the Qur'an speaks for itself and that people whose minds are shaped by a violent foundational text will likely be inclined toward violence.

Now, there is no doubt that the Qur'an contains much that is disgusting by modern liberal standards. And it is disturbing that movements emphasizing jihad against the infidel have gained strength. But the Qur'an does *not* speak for itself. The vast majority of Muslims only make heavily mediated contact with the Qur'an. A typical Muslim is unlikely to be literate in classical Arabic, and using translations is not an everyday practice. Ordinary Muslims depend heavily on their local religious scholars, Sufi orders and similar brotherhoods, officially sanctioned clergy, and other mediating institutions. They hold the Qur'an sacred, but their understanding of what Islam demands comes through their local religious culture. Their interpretations are filtered through the mainstream legal traditions and the unexciting, nonviolent needs of everyday life. Even fundamentalists, who ostensibly strip away the accretions of tradition to go back to the original texts, do no such thing. They sanctify diverse modern readings by imagining a return to purity.

This is not to join in the whitewashing of Islam as a "religion of peace." Violent forms of religiosity are available to Muslims today, as are moderate ways of political engagement. Jihad is a legitimate strand within Islam, no less than quietism. But no argument that presents violent verses in the Qur'an and declares that therefore faithful Muslims must be inclined toward violence deserves to be taken seriously.

I would like to ignore Harris's views, especially since he did not do even the elementary work of consulting a few scholarly sources before writing his polemic. But he appears to be popular among secular people. Many secularists who are impressed with Harris urge a similar view of Islam. So I worry that, if such attitudes are widespread, it means that many Western secular people harbor grave misunderstandings about Islam, and perhaps even about religion in general. It is precisely an uncompromisingly secular view of religion that should prevent us from going on a quest for a true Islam. The Qur'an is often incoherent, obscure, and archaic—its various, conflicting meanings arise from the interpretive activities of communities that consider it sacred and try to make sense of it in terms of their present needs. Devout Muslims must believe in a true Islam that is the measure of compliance and deviance, a divine reality revealed by the Qur'an. Muslim religious scholars must strive for orthodoxy and keep complaining about how even Muslims are ignorant of the true faith. Those of us who do not accept revelation, however, need not go in search of an idealized, true Islam. We should give up those habits of thought that prompt us to seek a well-defined true faith, now to condemn as barbaric rather than to endorse as divine. Religion is a human activity, and what deserve our attention are the varieties of faith revealed in actual practice.

Secular humanists have been very supportive of science and critiques of Islam; they have stood up for freedom of inquiry. And as a godless infidel, a scientist, and a critic of Islam, I am grateful for this support. But we secularists also have our blind spots, our episodes of intellectual laziness. Accepting the framework of a "true Islam" is one such mistake. We can do better.

Taner Edis is an associate professor of physics at Truman State University. His latest book is An Illusion of Harmony: Science and Religion in Islam *(Prometheus Books, 2007).*

WHO PUBLISHED THE NEW TESTAMENT?

David Trobisch

In the fall of 2000, Oxford University Press published *The First Edition of the New Testament*, the English version of my German postdoctoral thesis. In it, I tried to determine when the New Testament was first published. I concentrated my efforts on studying the manuscript tradition. The result was surprising and differed considerably from the conclusions drawn in the classic studies by Alfred Loisy (1891), Theodor Zahn (1888–1892), Adolf von Harnack (1914), and Hans von Campenhausen (1968).

The existing early specimens of the New Testament feature a closed selection of twenty-seven writings arranged in the same sequence and displaying uniform titles with very few variants. They were produced in the form of bound manuscripts and employ a unique system to mark sacred terms, the so-called *nomina sacra*. These features indicate that the New Testament is a carefully edited publication, rather than the product of a gradual process that lasted for centuries. Instead, it was edited and published by specific people at a very specific time and place. Because its first documented readers are the church fathers Irenaeus, Tertullian, Clement of Alexandria, Origen, and Tatian—all of whom wrote at the end of the second and the beginning of

78

the third centuries—the New Testament must have been published before 180 C.E.

In the ten years since the first publication of my book in German, numerous reviews have been written, and many colleagues have tested my theory. They either liked it or they hated it, but to my knowledge no one has been able to point out a serious flaw in either the evidence evaluated or the conclusions drawn. So, I will assume that the theory has withstood the test of time and take the next step of interpreting the New Testament as a publication of the second century.

I will also assume that the New Testament contains forgeries, an assumption shared by the majority of historical scholars. A forgery is an authoritative document that lies about its true authorship. Books of the New Testament widely regarded as forgeries include 1 Timothy, 2 Timothy, Titus, and 2 Peter. These letters appear to have been written by the apostles Paul and Peter, although they were actually authored by someone else. Whoever designed them intended to deceive readers about their true authorship.

If you cannot find it in your heart to look at the New Testament as a publication of the second century that contains forgeries, then the following deliberations are not for you. But, if you are willing to entertain the idea that the New Testament, like any other book, was published by a person or a group of people, then you might be interested in asking the question: *Who* published the first edition of the New Testament?

THE CASE FOR FORGERY

To demonstrate the typical characteristics of published forgeries, consider two examples: the letters of Ignatius of Antioch (ca. 35–107) and the ninth-century *Pseudo-Isidorian Decretals*, a once-influential collection of authoritative documents.

The letters of Ignatius have come to us in several editions. The most successful edition, as measured by the number of extant manuscripts, contains thirteen letters. Contemporary scholarship, however, has reached a consensus that six letters are forgeries, while the other seven letters represent expanded versions of the original letters. The six spurious letters were written by the same person who added to the original ones.

In recent years, this inventive person has been identified through the work of Dieter Hagedorn as a certain Julian, a fourth-century Arian Christian and the author of a commentary on the book of Job. He is also the compiler of a much larger forgery, the *Apostolic Constitutions*. In this work, Clement, the legendary third successor to Peter as bishop of Rome, records what the apostles said. They speak in first person. Julian most likely worked in Syria and published between 350 and 380 C.E.

The *Pseudo-Isidorian Decretals* contain more than ten thousand excerpts, combining authentic documents with spurious material. They were first introduced in the trials against Catholic clerics in northeastern France during the ninth century. The function of this collection is to prove that bishops are under the jurisdiction of the pope and do not have to answer to provincial synods or secular authorities. In addition to canons issued by synods and councils since Nicea, the *Pseudo-Isidorian Decretals* contain papal letters, so-called decretals. They begin with letters attributed to Clement of Rome and continue on up through Gregory II, an account of whose council of 721 forms the last piece of the collection. The compiler introduces himself as Isidor Mercator, suggesting to naïve readers that the author is Isidor of Sevilla, the famous medieval bishop and influential scholar. The true author has yet to be identified.

I chose these two examples to show that it is sometimes possible to describe the place, time, and historical circumstances of published collections that contain forgeries. Now, to determine the provenance and authorship of the *Four-Gospel-Book* (the New Testament), careful study shows the following three areas to be especially promising in their potential to yield relevant information: (1) editorial notes to the readers, (2) the first documented users of the collection, and (3) geographical information contained in the forgeries.

Editorial notes to readers. Once scholarly investigators made the connection between Julian's commentary on Job and the *Apostolic Constitutions* and interpolated letters of Ignatius, it was possible to describe the theological position of the author and the interest of the editor.

A similar structure is found in the New Testament. The Gospel of John ends with the following note to readers: "The disciple whom Jesus loved . . . was the one who had reclined next to Jesus at the supper and had said, 'Lord, who is it that is going to betray you?' . . . This is the disciple who is testifying to these things and has written them, and we know that his testimony is true" (John 21:20–24 NRSV).

In this sentence, the editors disclose their source to the reader. This is not unusual in the New Testament. Comparable editorial notes can be found in the introductions to Luke, Acts, and Revelation. A modern rendition might sound like: "We used a manuscript written by the favorite disciple of Jesus, the one who was next to him at the Last Supper. We trust that his account of the events is authentic." A note to the reader always has an unwritten subtext: "There are other books around that tell the story differently, but we think *we* got it right." Readers of the canonical collection will have read or at least noticed three Gospels before they encounter John's Gospel. And they may have questions about why some of the stories are told quite differently in John. The editorial note at the end of John invites them to read the fourth Gospel as an authoritative commentary on the first three, a commentary written from the perspective of an eyewitness who tells the readers what really happened.

The last sentence of John, however, goes one step further: "But there are also many other things that Jesus did; if every one of them were written down, I suppose that the world itself could not contain the books that would be written" (John 21:25 NRSV). The authorial voice shifts from the first-person plural "we know" to first-person singular "I suppose." And this sentence does not refer to only one author and one manuscript; instead, it talks about "books" in the plural. The reader of John will have just finished reading the fourth account of "things that Jesus did." A modern rendition of this sentence may sound like: "If everything Jesus did was written down, I suppose that the world could not contain all the books that would have to be published. Four books are plenty!" The last sentence of John does not refer only to the Gospel according to John; it refers to the Gospel collection as a whole. It may have been written by the publisher of the *Four-Gospel-Book*.

If this reading is correct, we can draw several conclusions about the publisher:

1. He is well known. Using the first person singular indicates that the *Four-Gospel-Book* was not published anonymously and that the first readers were aware of the name of the publisher. If this was a famous person of the time, we have hope that we would recognize his name even today.

2. Whoever wrote this sentence used his authority to add John to the canon as a witness to the synoptic gospels.

3. One of the major disagreements between the fourth Gospel and the first three is the date of Jesus's death. Whereas the synoptic gospels have Jesus celebrate the Passover meal with his disciples the evening before he dies, John has Jesus die on the afternoon before Passover. In the second century, Asia Minor followed the Johannine tradition, commemorating Jesus's death on the day before Passover no matter what day of the week this happened to be. Rome, on the other hand, always commemorated Jesus's death on a Friday. This led to differences in the fasting observances and gave rise to a well-documented conflict of the second century, the so-called Easter Controversy. By publishing John together with the synoptics, the publisher indicates that he is aware of the discrepancy but tolerates both positions.

The first documented users. The *Pseudo-Isidorian Decretals* surfaced first in northeastern France during the second half of the ninth century. They provided critical evidence in trials concerning clerics by insisting that bishops had to answer only to the pope. Most forgeries originate close to the location where they are first used; therefore, the first documented users provide important clues concerning the date, location, and intent of a forgery.

Like no other book of the New Testament, the book of Acts offers a view into the whole collection. Being the second volume of Luke's work, it provides a link to the *Four-Gospel-Book*. In its first half, Acts introduces the authors of the General Letters: Peter, John, James, and Jude; in the second half, it introduces Paul, the author of the other New Testament letter collection. In addition, Acts provides information that makes it possible to identify Luke, the author of the Gospel, as the doctor who travels with Paul and to identify Mark as someone close to

Peter *and* Paul. This "canon consciousness" suggests that the book of Acts was composed at a later date than is typically thought; this theory is supported by the first attestation of the book around 180 C.E. The first writer to quote from and make references to Acts is Irenaeus, who uses Acts extensively to refute the heretical theologian Marcion (ca. 110–160) in the third book of his *Against Heresies.*

Marcionite Christianity followed the lead of Paul and opposed the Jerusalem-based leadership of James and his associates. The Marcionite Bible contained only one Gospel, which was close to (but not identical with) the canonical Gospel according to Luke; in addition to the Gospel, it contained ten letters of Paul, but Hebrews and the Pastorals were not included. Irenaeus uses Acts to argue that anyone who accepts the authority of the Gospel according to Luke would also have to accept the authority of the second volume, the book of Acts.

Forgeries usually originate in close proximity to their first users. Therefore, it is very likely that the book of Acts, in the form we read it today, was produced to assist the emerging Catholic Church in its struggle against Marcionite Christianity. This is also true for the New Testament as a whole. Whoever selected the eight authors whose writings are collected in the New Testament tried to give as much representation to Paul as he did to the Jerusalem leadership. The letters of Paul are balanced by a collection of letters from Peter, John, and Jesus's brothers James and Jude. The gospel of Paul (Luke) is offset by the Gospels of Matthew and John. Mark, who is portrayed as being close to both Peter (1 Peter 5:13) and Paul (Col. 4:10), serves as a role model to the readers, encouraging them not to make a choice between Peter and Paul.

Geographical information in the forgeries. The vast majority of New Testament interpreters assume that 1 Timothy, 2 Timothy, Titus, and 2 Peter are forgeries. 1 Timothy and 2 Timothy are both written to Ephesus; 2 Peter presents itself as the second letter written to the same addressees of 1 Peter ("This is now, beloved, the second letter I am writing to you" [2 Peter 3:1]). These addressees live all over Asia Minor ("To the exiles of the Dispersion in Pontus, Galatia, Cappadocia, Asia, and Bithynia" [1 Peter 1:1]). 1 Timothy is written from an undisclosed location, but 2 Timothy (cf. 2 Tim 1:17) and 2 Peter (implied from 1 Peter 5:13: "Your sister church in Babylon") are both written from Rome. And the mention of Crete in Titus (1:5) suggests to the reader of the New Testament a link to the book of Acts, in which Paul travels to Rome by way of Crete (Acts 27).

These four forgeries display an interest in Rome and Asia Minor. Letter collections published in antiquity usually drew from the archive of the addressee. Considering that 2 Timothy is presented as the testament of Paul and 2 Peter as the testament of Peter—both having been written in Rome and sent to Asia Minor—one should conclude that the authority of these writings would depend heavily on what the church leadership in Asia had to say about their authenticity. It seems more likely that the forgeries originated in Asia Minor than in Rome.

THE PUBLISHER OF THE NEW TESTAMENT

If one considers the note to the readers of the Gospel collection (John 21:25), the canonical awareness of Acts, and the prominence of Asia Minor and Rome in the New Testament's forged letters, some characteristics of the ideal publisher of the New Testament in the middle of the second century become clear:

1. He was a well-known person of the time.

2. He held authority among Catholic Christians in Rome and Asia Minor.
3. He was a person who would add credibility to the Gospel of John and to the other Johannine writings of the New Testament (1, 2, 3 John and Revelation).
4. He displayed a tolerant attitude toward the Easter Controversy.
5. He opposed Marcionite Christianity.
6. He was a person with experience in publishing.

Polycarp of Smyrna fulfills all these criteria. He was a bishop earlier than 110 C.E., when Ignatius addressed a letter to him, and he died sometime between 155 and 167 C.E. He certainly was a prominent person of the time (1) and carried authority with Catholic Christians in Asia Minor (2). He is described as a disciple of John by Irenaeus, and his esteemed position would have added credibility to the publication of Johannine material (3). Polycarp of Smyrna was chosen by the congregations in Asia Minor to represent them in the Easter Controversy. He was sent to Rome to negotiate with his counterpart, Bishop Anicetus. They agreed to disagree. This sequence of events matches the position described in the covering note to the *Four-Gospel-Book* (John 21:25) (4). Furthermore, Polycarp is reported by Irenaeus to have opposed Marcion to his face, calling him the firstborn of Satan (5). Last but not least, Polycarp had experience in publishing. He assembled and distributed the first edition of the Letters of Ignatius.

The time frame is set by Anicetus, who became bishop in 156–157 C.E., and by the latest possible date for Polycarp's martyrdom, 168 C.E.

I will conclude these considerations with a bold statement:

The New Testament was published by Polycarp of Smyrna between 156 and 168 C.E.

THE CORROBORATING EVIDENCE

Goethe. In 1774, a pamphlet was published in Germany under the title *Goetter, Helden und Wieland: Eine Farce* (*Gods, Heroes and Wieland: A Farce*). In this booklet, the author poked fun at a highly recognized poet of the time, Christoph Martin Wieland. Although the book was published anonymously, the author left a clue on the title page that made it possible to identify him. The title page was typeset so the name of the true author, W. Goethe, was contained in the first letter or letters of every line.

GOETter

HElden und

Wieland

The extra in 2 Timothy 4:9–20. Like Goethe's title page, 2 Timothy 4:9–20 may contain the names of the publisher and forger of this letter. The passage contains thirteen names: Demas, Crescens, Titus, Luke, Mark, Tychicus, Carpus, Alexander, Prisca, Aquila, Onesiphorus, Erastus, and Trophimus. Of these, all but two are mentioned elsewhere in the New Testament. Forgeries often repeat information from genuine material to create credibility; interpreters are well advised to concentrate on the additional material, the "extra." In this case, the two names, Carpus and Crescens, should command our interest. Carpus could easily be interpreted as referring to Bishop Polycarp. But who is Crescens?

A letter of Polycarp to the Philippians has survived. It served as the introduction to Polycarp's edition of the Letters of Ignatius. In this letter, he thanks his secretary and gives his name:

"These things I have written to you with the help of Crescens. I have recommended him to you and I recommend him to you again. For he has acted blamelessly among us, and I believe also among you." Although this argument cannot carry the burden of proof, it is a nice example of corroborating evidence.

Further Reading

Fuhrmann, Horst. *Einfluß und Verbreitung der pseudoisidorischen Fälschungen: Von ihrem Auftauchen bis in die neuere Zeit.* Schriften der Monumenta Germaniae historica 24, 1. Stuttgart: Hiersemann, 1972. Three volumes.

Hagedorn, Dieter, ed. *Der Hiobkommentar des Arianers Julian. Patristische Texte und Studien 14.* Berlin and New York: de Gruyter, 1973.

Schoedel, William R. *Ignatius of Antioch.* Philadelphia: Fortress, 1985.

Trobisch, David. *Die Entstehung der Paulusbriefsammlung: Studien zu den Anfängen der christlichen Publizistik. Novum Testamentum et Orbis Antiquus,* 10. Freiburg. Schweiz: Universitätsverlag; Göttingen: Vandenhoeck, 1989.

Trobisch, David. *The First Edition of the New Testament.* New York: Oxford University Press, 2000.

David Trobisch is currently the Throckmorton-Hayes Professor of New Testament Language and Literature at Bangor Theological Seminary in Maine. He has also taught at the University of Heidelberg, Missouri State University, and Yale Divinity School. He is the author of several books, including The First Edition of the New Testament *(Oxford University Press, 2000) and* Paul's Collection of Letters: Exploring the Origins *(Fortress Press, 1994).*

WHERE CAN GOD ACT? A LOOK AT QUANTUM THEOLOGY

Victor J. Stenger

THE CLOCKWORK UNIVERSE

In 1687, Isaac Newton published *The Mathematical Principles of Natural Philosophy*, now referred to simply as *Principia*, which many scholars say is the greatest work of science ever produced. Newtonian mechanics provided the means for predicting the motion of every body in the universe with what appears to be unlimited precision. All you need to know is the mass of the body, its initial position and momentum, and the net force acting on it, and the laws of motion allow you to calculate the position and velocity of the body at any time.

Newton insisted that he was demonstrating the work of divine providence in nature. However, his discoveries conflicted profoundly with traditional Christian teaching. If the motion of every body in the universe is fully determined by Newton's laws of motion and force, then there is nothing for God to do beyond the creation—no reason to step in to perform miracles or answer prayers. Even before Newton, philosophers had begun to view the universe as a vast machine. With Newton, that picture seemed to be confirmed. We all live in a *clockwork universe* with everything predetermined.

As a consequence, a new concept of God arose, a new theology called "deism," in which a perfect, all-knowing, all-powerful God created the universe and its laws, then left it alone to carry on by itself. Whatever purpose God had in creating the universe, that purpose is built-in and inevitable, since every event is already predetermined. Indeed, only if God were imperfect would he need to intervene to change the course of events.

This period in Western history, when science and rational thinking began to challenge superstition and appeals to religious authority, is called the Age of the Enlightenment. The central tenet of the Enlightenment was Newtonian determinism. Many of America's Founding Fathers—including Thomas Jefferson, Benjamin Franklin, James Madison, and Thomas Paine—were deists. Some European thinkers saw no need even for a deist God, and for the first time in the history of Christendom, atheism became a respectable alternative.

The main objection to the clockwork universe is its implication that humans do not possess free will. This means that we are not responsible for our actions and possess no power of choice. Not only does this contradict the central religious doctrines of sin and atonement, it poses real problems for secular society. If a person is not responsible for his acts, what basis is there for punishing or rewarding those acts? Besides, most people have the innate conviction that they possess the freedom to act self-consciously no matter what scientists or philosophers may say.

In *Emile, ou l'education*, Jean-Jacques Rousseau's fictional Vicar of Savoyard chastises philosophers to recognize that something may be true even if they cannot understand it. Such is the case, the vicar says, for the free-acting immaterial mind, which is a fact immediately perceived in his "inner light." Rousseau led the way out of Enlightenment deism and atheism by teaching a theology in which everything natural is good and evil is humanity's doing (although the notion of the "noble savage" was not Rousseau's doing).

NATURAL THEOLOGY

The Enlightenment did not bring about the demise of Christianity. Rather, Christianity began to adapt to its own brand of deism, using the metaphor of mechanism and the wonders of science to extol the glory and power of God while assuming the existence of a parallel world of mind or spirit that was not constrained by Newton's laws. Furthermore, nature itself ostensibly offered proof of God's existence.

William Paley eloquently articulated this view in his 1802 book *Natural Theology*, in which he introduced the famous watchmaker analogy for God. Paley tells of walking on the heath and finding a stone and a watch. While the stone is easily viewed as an object formed by natural forces, the same is not true of the watch, which is clearly an artifact. Paley then compares the watch with biological structures such as the human eye and argues that the eye cannot possibly be the product of any purely natural process. It calls out for a designer, and that designer, of course, is God.

Charles Darwin, who was assigned the same rooms at Cambridge that Paley occupied a generation earlier, was very impressed by Paley's argument. But ultimately he was unconvinced and in 1859 published *On the Origin of Species*, laying out the evidence that living organisms evolve by a process of random mutations and natural selection (a process that Alfred Russel Wallace had independently also discovered).

Even today, Christians are told by their preachers to look at the beauty and complexity of the world about them, smell the flowers, peer through telescopes into the heavens, and bear witness to God's creative artifacts in nature. The *argument from design* remains the most common scientific argument theists give for their beliefs, despite the fact that evolution by natural selection is now solidly confirmed as the mechanism by which complex living organisms develop from simpler forms.

Of course, most fundamentalist Christians refuse to accept evolution because it conflicts with the Bible. These dedicated faithful represent a strong political force in the United States, but they have so far failed in their efforts to remake science so that Christian principles take precedence over established scientific methodology.

THE PREMISE KEEPERS

The antiscientists do not concern me in this essay. I am far more interested in and respectful of those theologians who accept the results of science and do not dispute the power of its meticulous procedures but make an honest attempt to reconcile it with God. In an earlier essay, which mainly focused on evolution theology, I referred to them as the "premise keepers." They include, among others, the particle physicist and Anglican priest John Polkinghorne, the biochemist and Anglican priest Arthur Peacocke, the biologist Kenneth Miller, the physicist and theologian Ian Barbour, the cosmologist and Quaker George Ellis, the physicist and theologian Willem Drees, and theologians John Haught and Nancey Murphy. Since many of the proposals I will discuss have appeared in the writings of several of these thinkers, I will generally not single out the views of individuals but rather seek out their common thread.

The problem of locating God's action has been the subject of a multiyear collaborative project between the Vatican Observatory and the Center for Theology and the Natural Sciences, located in Berkeley. Five volumes of proceedings edited by Center director (and premise keeper) Robert John Russell have been produced. A whole issue of *Zygon, the Journal of Religion and Science* was recently devoted to the question. A number of books of varying scholarly quality have also been published.

The premise keepers, who are almost all Christians, recognize that the deist God, even in the dual model of matter and mind, is not the Christian God. So they seek ways for a God to act that is both consistent with Christian tradition and does not violate natural laws. These acts might be in response to earnest prayers or the need to fix some sequence of events that has gone off course just because of the large amount of random, unpremeditated chance that evidently exists in our universe.

Note that the premise keepers do not allow for miracles if these violate laws of nature. As Polkinghorne put it, if God worked against the laws of nature it would be God acting against God, the presumed author of those laws. So it is not simply a matter of saying "God is God, he can do anything he wants to do." Whatever actions the premise keepers propose for God to take in the current world beyond his actions at creation should be consistent with the laws of nature—at least as we perceive them on the human scale. This is not a restriction on God; it is a restriction on the possible theories of God that theologians can consider while being consistent with science and avoiding the need for God to act against his own creation. What may appear as a miracle is just an unusual event, not a violation of natural law.

Another restriction on theologians is that their God theory must allow for human free will, which is fundamental to Christian belief. This means that God's actions can, in principle, be thwarted by human actions. Somehow theologians have to arrange it so that God's actions are beyond the reach of the human capability to undo.

As with the clockwork universe, theologians must grope for a place for God to act in the course of evolution. Since we still do not understand how life originally came about on Earth, anyone is free to propose that God initiated the process. However, even if God did create life, he could not simply then turn it over to natural selection the way the deist God turned over physics to Newtonian determinism. Consider the matter of the development of the human race. Evolution tells us that we are the result of an enormous number of random mutations that have occurred since life began on Earth four billion years ago. If, as Christianity and other religions teach, God created the universe with a special place and plan for humanity, then he would have had to intervine countless times along the way—every time there was a mutation on the path to *Homo sapiens*—to make sure that we evolved. Such actions may be indistinguishable from evolution but would constitute a form of intelligent design inconsistent with the more parsimonious evolutionary principle that random mutations are sufficient to provide the genetic changes needed for natural selection to operate.

Several premise keepers have proposed that God did not care whether humans evolved or not. For his own reasons, he set things up the way he did, with many paths to some final end that need not include humanity. That's possible, but such a God must then be reconciled with the traditional Christian teaching and widespread human belief that we are special and central to God's plan for the universe.

Nevertheless, evolution by natural selection did theologians a great favor. By including chance in the development of life well before the twentieth century, when chance became a major player in physics and cosmology, evolution blew a big hole in the clockwork universe and relegated the Enlightenment deist God to history. Living organisms are not predetermined after all. They are a consequence of random chance and natural selection.

UNCERTAINTY

The Newtonian clockwork universe has never been a problem for the vast majority of believers to whom the name Newton is more likely to bring up an association with a tasty fig cookie than laws of motion. Nevertheless, prior to the twentieth century, theologians still had to grapple with the problem of finding a place for God to act within the framework of the clockwork universe. Natural theology just swept this under the rug. Since there is no compelling evidence that God acts anywhere, the simplest conclusion is that he does not exist. However, theologians would soon lose their jobs if there were no God theories to speculate about. And here is where modern quantum mechanics provides a playing field for speculation.

Perhaps the most important innovation in quantum mechanics is the *uncertainty principle*, introduced in 1927 by Werner Heisenberg, which says that the momentum and position of a body cannot be simultaneously measured with unlimited precision. (Except at speeds near the speed of light, momentum can usually be approximated as the product of the mass and velocity of a body.)

We saw above that Newton's laws of motion provide a means for predicting the motion of a body when we know the initial position and velocity of the body and forces acting on it. This was the basis of the clockwork universe in which everything that happens is predetermined. The uncertainty principle seems to rescue us from determinism. For example, there is no way for a physicist to predict with any reasonable accuracy the motion of a free electron initially confined within a volume the size of an atom. The uncertainty in the electron's velocity by virtue of its position being so well known is one million meters per second with random direction! Six seconds later, the electron can be anywhere within a volume the size of Earth. By contrast, the uncertainty in the velocity of a body of mass equal to one gram confined to a cubic centimeter is 5×10^{-30} meters per second, and the motion of such a particle can be predicted with great accuracy.

Of course, the fact that a physicist cannot predict something does not necessarily mean it is not predetermined. But let us assume this is an ontological, not just an epistemological, fact so that we are not back to the Enlightenment deistic God.

Does this open up a place for God to act, poking his finger in so that the electron goes where he wants rather than, as implied by quantum mechanics, almost any place at random? Many premise keepers have suggested so. In the case of the electron confined to a tiny region of space, God could direct the motion of that electron to where he wants it within the limits of the uncertainty principle. But note that to do so, he would in fact be *violating* the uncertainty principle, just as he violated evolution in the example discussed above. Of course, being God, he can do that. But so long as God limited himself to placing the electron at a precise location within a volume the size of Earth in six seconds, humans would not be able to detect it, just as poking his finger into evolution would be indistinguishable from randomness. All this appears possible—God *could* be behaving in this way—and the only argument against it is once again parsimony.

Every gram of matter contains a trillion trillion electrons, protons, and neutrons. This means that a deity would have to somehow maintain control over countless events taking place at the submicroscopic level over extended periods of time. The prospect of God micromanaging all these particles throughout the universe has not appealed to many theologians. The premise keepers are looking for ways for God to act on the everyday scale of human experience, where that action is meaningful to humanity. If God is to use quantum mechanics to act in the universe, those actions must be amplified by some mechanism, and, furthermore, they must involve large-scale phenomena that are otherwise not predetermined.

BUTTERFLIES AND CHAOS

Some premise keepers have proposed that the amplification mechanism might be found in the so-called butterfly effect, discovered in 1960 by meteorologist Edward Lorenz. Running a model of the atmosphere on one of the primitive computers of the day, Lorenz found that the model was very sensitive to tiny changes in the input data, such as when he entered a number that had been rounded off in printing from the actual number inside the computer. It was as if a butterfly flapping its wings could change the weather days ahead.

Since then, this phenomenon, dubbed "chaos," has been studied extensively with experiments and computer simulations. We have seen that Newtonian mechanics allows the prediction of the motion of a body with unlimited accuracy, at least for large-scale phenomena. It can do this as well for a system of two bodies. But when you move to three bodies, it becomes impossible because of the mathematical complexity required to describe all possibilities and the apparent impossibility of an exact solution. Approximation techniques, such as *perturbation theory*, enable physicists to make useful calculations for systems of a few bodies that interact with one another weakly, for example, the planets and other bodies in the solar system. But even this fails when the bodies strongly interact.

Of course, it is hopeless to calculate the detailed motion of the trillion trillion molecules in a gram of familiar matter. Instead, physicists use statistical techniques to calculate the average behavior of such systems. With the highly developed theory of statistical mechanics, many of the gross properties of the gases, liquids, and solids of normal and laboratory experience can be computed, but these systems must be in thermal equilibrium (constant temperature throughout) or not too far from it. This stratagem fails for many multibody systems that are far from equilibrium, for example, Earth's atmosphere with its turbulence and strong interactions with land and sea.

Computer simulations have shown that the butterfly effect and other unexpected phenomena are associated with systems that have three basic characteristics:

1. *Nonlinearity.* A linear system is one whose output response to a stimulus is proportional to the stimulus. For nonlinear systems this is not the case.

2. *Energy dissipation.* The system must have a means of losing energy, such as friction.

3. *External driving force.* An outside force must act on the system.

A simple example of a system that meets these characteristics is the damped, driven pendulum. A pendulum will respond linearly to a slight push, but its response becomes nonlinear as the push gets harder. Add damping, and the pendulum behaves chaotically.

Chaotic systems appear to behave unpredictably. At least there is no known mathematical technique that enables one to go from the initial conditions to the final results. However, for a system on the everyday human scale, individual bodies such as air molecules inside the system obey Newtonian mechanics. The apparent unpredictability of a chaotic system is the result of our own limited knowledge of the initial conditions. When we do computer simulations on chaotic systems, we can predict the outcome even if we can't calculate it by traditional mathematical means. All we need to do is run the simulation once and see where the system ends up. Then, as long as we run it again from the same initial point (taking care to avoid rounding errors), we will end up at the same final point. For these reasons, we refer to the chaos associated with nonlinear systems as "deterministic chaos." Indeed, quantum systems, which are not deterministic in most interpretations, are linear and so do not exhibit this variety of chaos. Attempts to develop a nonlinear version of quantum mechanics have so far failed. In fact, linearity lies behind many quantum effects, such as "entanglement."

The primary characteristic of chaotic systems is their sensitivity to initial conditions. The uncertainty principle of quantum mechanics could in principle result in a large-scale, otherwise deterministic, chaotic system such as a pendulum or an unpredictable atmosphere because of our inability to set the initial conditions accurately.

Several theologians have proposed chaos as the means for amplifying God's action from the quantum level to the macroscopic level. Working within the uncertainty principle so that he breaks no laws of physics, God would have to change the initial conditions of a chaotic system to affect the outcome.

This means that God, knowing how to do Newtonian mechanics better than we do and presumably having the best computer in heaven at his disposal, can thus obtain his desired outcome. He simply chooses the initial conditions that lead deterministically to the desired result.

Christian schoolmaster Timothy Sansbury has pointed to three problems with this scenario for God's action. First, a significant time delay is involved in the kinds of chaotic amplification systems we might consider; for example, it might take several days for the butterfly effect to change the weather. Second, it is not clear that dramatic changes can be effected, such as bringing rain in response to farmers' prayers. It certainly would not move fast enough to change the course of a tornado heading straight for your house or end a storm endangering a ship at sea.

Third, during the time that a chaotic system is working its way from initial conditions to final outcome, something might happen to change that course. This may not be a butterfly flapping its wings, but since we are assuming God gave humans free will, some human might take an action that God did not anticipate when he made his adjustment to the initial conditions. For example, that human might decide at the last moment to get into his carbon monoxide-emitting SUV and drive to Las Vegas, changing the chemical composition of the atmosphere just enough to thwart God's plan.

In short, it does not seem that quantum mechanics, even with chaotic amplification, provides a place for God to act that avoids violating laws of nature or human free will.

A GOD WHO PLAYS DICE

We have seen that the Enlightenment's deistic God who created the universe with everything predetermined is not viable if we accept the view of most physicists and philosophers that quantum mechanics implies only a *statistical* determinism. This is certainly the way quantum mechanics is currently applied. The same equations of motion that appear in classical Newtonian mechanics can be used to predict the average motion of an ensemble of particles but not that of individual particles. This is not to say that the motions of particles are random. Somehow their motions are constrained to yield the calculated average. Indeed, the exact statistical distribution giving the range of deviations from average motion can also be calculated.

Now, it remains possible that the motions of particles *are* predetermined, and we simply have not yet discovered the underlying principles. This was the suggestion made in the 1950s by David Bohm—that there are "hidden variables" governing the behavior of individual particles. The pursuit of these hidden variables has led to some interesting developments that have been given mystical interpretations, which I covered in my 1995 book, *The Unconscious Quantum*. For our present purposes, let me just note that no evidence for hidden variables has been uncovered, and the world of quantum mechanics continues to appear indeterministic. And, if Bohm turns out to be correct and everything is predetermined after all, we are back to the very non-Christian "God" of Enlightenment deism.

We are rapidly narrowing the list of possible gods consistent with science. We can with some confidence eliminate the Enlightenment's deist God. A personal God who acts within quantum uncertainty, possibly amplified by chaos, to change the outcome of events in the natural world remains possible but unnecessary. This would seem to leave open only the possibility of the God to which Einstein strongly objected, the God who "plays dice."

As mentioned, several premise keepers have proposed such a god. This is a different kind of deist God who creates the universe and its laws and leaves it alone to run itself according to those laws, but allows for an extra ingredient of chance that he does not control. Rather, his purposes are served regardless of the particular path the universe and life take among the countless possible paths available to them. This, of course, leaves ample room for human free will and a great amount of possible creativity, given the way simple systems are able to evolve into more complex forms naturally and without outside help.

Now, while Christian apologists can find ways to fit the chaos deity into their always-flexible interpretations of scripture and religious doctrines, this God is not one to pray to and is hardly worth anyone's time to worship.

Furthermore, modern physics and cosmology make even the chaos deity, and indeed any creator, unlikely. This follows from the following observations:

1. No laws of physics were violated when the universe came into existence.
2. Several detailed theoretical papers have been published by reputable scientists in reputable journals that provide various scenarios by which our universe could have arisen spontaneously from nothing but the quantum characteristics of a vacuum, in a way consistent with all existing knowledge.
3. Something is *more natural* than nothing. A state of nothing will tend to undergo a phase transformation to a state of something. The universe appears to be an evolving state of "frozen nothing."
4. The laws of physics are those that would be expected to exist if the universe arose from nothing. By "nothing" I refer to a state of complete disorder—no matter, no energy, no structure and, most significantly, no information.
5. The structure of the universe could have evolved from simpler systems, mostly by chance.
6. The universe at its beginning was in a state of total disorder

and zero information. Order and information evolved later. Thus the universe retains no memory of a creator—or of that creator's intentions.

In short, a creator who plays dice may have existed. But that universe is evolving by itself without any divine purpose or plan provided by that creator.

Further Reading

Clayton, Philip. *Mind and Emergence: From Quantum to Consciousness.* Oxford: Oxford University Press, 2004.
Haught, John F. *God After Darwin.* Boulder, Col.: Westview Press, 2000.
Miller, Kenneth R. *Finding Darwin's God: A Scientist's Search for a Common Ground Between God and Evolution.* New York: Harper Collins, 1999.
O'Murchu, Diarmuid. *Quantum Theology: Spiritual Implications of the New Physics.* New York: Crossroad Publishing Company, 1997.
Peters, Ted, and Nathan Hallanger, eds. *God's Action in Nature's World: Essays in Honour of Robert John Russell.* Aldershot, England: Ashgate, 2006.
Polkinghorne, John. "The Metaphysics of Divine Action," in *Chaos and Complexity: Scientific Perspectives on Divine Action,* edited by R.J. Russell, N. Murphy, and A. Peacocke. Vatican City: Vatican Observatory, 1995.
———. *Belief in God in the Age of Science.* New Haven and London: Yale University Press, 1998.
———. *Quantum Physics and Theology: An Unexpected Kinship.* New Haven and London: Yale University Press, 2007.
Sansbury, Timothy. "The False Promise of Quantum Mechanics," *Zygon* 42, no. 1 (March 2007).
Stenger, Victor J. *The Unconscious Quantum: Metaphysics in Modern Physics and Cosmology.* Amherst, N.Y.: Prometheus Books, 1995.
———. "The Premise Keepers," *Free Inquiry* 23, no. 3 (Summer 2003).
———. *Has Science Found God?* Amherst, N.Y.: Prometheus Books, 2003.
———. *The Comprehensible Cosmos: Where Do the Laws of Physics Come From?* Amherst, N.Y.: Prometheus Books, 2006.
———. *God: The Failed Hypothesis. How Science Shows That God Does Not Exist.* Amherst, N.Y.: Prometheus Books, 2007.

Victor J. Stenger's New York Times *best-seller,* God: The Failed Hypothesis—How Science Shows that God Does Not Exist, *is now out in paperback with a foreword by Christopher Hitchens and a new postscript by the author. Stenger is an adjunct professor of philosophy at the University of Colorado and professor emeritus of physics and astronomy at the University of Hawaii.*

HOPE, DESPAIR, DREAD, AND RELIGION

Ronald A. Lindsay

Secular humanists often assert that they offer something more than critiquing religion, that they have a "positive outlook" and offer affirmative alternatives to religion. When I encounter statements of this sort, I admit I am sometimes puzzled—particularly when what follows these words is some recitation of vague principles to which religious individuals can subscribe as easily as humanists. How many religious persons, for example, would claim they are against the dignity and worth of every individual—something often cited as a humanist value?

I do believe that humanists have a perspective and a method they can bring to bear on issues other than critical examination of religion, in particular moral issues. However, we humanists need to do a better job in explaining what it is exactly that the humanist perspective and method can contribute to the discussion of such issues. Repeatedly invoking vague principles and values will not suffice.

That is a general observation. Let me turn to some specific points, which relate to humanist alternatives to belief in the afterlife. In a recent insightful editorial (*FI*, February/March 2010), Paul Kurtz correctly identified the hope for immortality as one of the principal motivations for religious belief. Empirical research seems to confirm this proposition, as some psychological studies show that heightened awareness of one's vulnerability to death tends to intensify belief in supernatural agents, at least for those who already have some level of belief.

However, I differ with my colleague, both with respect to his explanation for the persistence of hope for an afterlife and his outline of the humanist alterative to false hopes of immortality. It is worth elaborating on these differences because they underscore some of the limitations and strengths of the humanist outlook.

Dr. Kurtz states that people are deluded by the false hope of an afterlife because they "lack the courage to become what they wish." These individuals fail to appreciate and take advantage of the many opportunities available to us today, which provide "virtually unlimited horizons for enjoyment and satisfaction." According to Dr. Kurtz, "our hopes are as unlimited as our dreams of a better tomorrow." Recognizing that opportunities are not the same for everyone in the world, he argues that we need to bring justice and material wealth to all the countries in the world. As he puts it, "The doctrine of divine salvation makes sense only in poor and/or unjust societies where people are hungry, sick, or repressed."

"Lack of courage" to pursue opportunities does not seem to me to be the best explanation for the persistence of hopes for eternal life. Leaving aside the question of whether religious believers would find such an explanation patronizing, if not insulting, it rings false. I have many religious acquaintances. None of them seems to suffer from a lack of courage to pursue his or her goals and ambitions. Indeed, some of them may be overly ambitious. And I'm not aware of any study that correlates timidity or reluctance to pursue opportunities with belief in an afterlife.

Regarding the notion that material well-being, social justice, and potential for personal achievement will cause people to give up belief in immortality, many scholars have predicted such an effect, including, perhaps, most notably, Karl Marx, who claimed that religion was a means of comforting the oppressed and would whither away once social justice was achieved and material conditions improved for all. However, there does not seem to be a straightforward cause-effect relationship between material well-being combined with agreeable social conditions and lack of religious belief. Granted, some of the more secular countries are also countries with a relative abundance of material goods, a secure social safety net, and a high degree of personal freedom, but there are other explanations for the secularization of these countries. In addition, countries such as the United States remain fairly religious despite material wealth, generally equitable (albeit imperfect) social conditions, and a high degree of personal autonomy. Furthermore, considering individuals as opposed to countries, material wealth, personal security, and expansive horizons do not always correlate with nonbelief. Many wealthy people are religious and believe in an afterlife. The Templeton Foundation was not established by a pauper.

I think we need to look deeper for the roots of the human longing for an afterlife. One can have material abundance, agreeable social conditions, and any number of opportunities for growth and achievement and still have an existential dread about death and other forms of irretrievable loss, such as permanent disability. This dread is triggered not only by concern over events that may affect one directly but also by the misfortunes that may befall one's loved ones. A father with religious tendencies who is watching a child slip away inexorably into death is not going to be dissuaded from embracing a hope to see his child again by being told to have the "courage to become what he wishes."

Dread is anticipatory. For losses that have already occurred, "despair" better describes the state of mind of those overcome by them. The same logic applies. For a mother with religious tendencies, a million dollars in annual income, multiple homes, and a richly rewarding career will not substitute for a child who was born disabled, suffered, and then died. In her despair, that mother may well turn to God and the hope of seeing her child again, and if she is religiously inclined already, reflection on the supposedly "unlimited horizons for enjoyment and satisfaction" available in the secular world will do little to persuade her to abandon that hope.

We need to accept the limits of the humanist outlook. Most of those who are religiously inclined and terrified of their own impending death or the death of a loved one will not stop yearning for an afterlife when they are reminded they have a virtually endless list of things to do. Or once had such a list. Or that they can take up eupraxsophy.

Does this mean we have nothing to offer those religious who believe in immortality? No, but we need to be clear about what it is we offer them and, importantly, when our offer should be made. The perceptive reader will note that throughout my discussion of religiously based hopes, I have emphasized the allure of such hopes to those who are already religious or have religious tendencies at the time of crisis. Atheists don't (usually) turn to God or pray for survival of their soul when confronted with their mortality. There are atheists in foxholes—but, on the other hand, one typically doesn't *become* an atheist while in a foxhole.

In other words, there is little chance that those who are religious will spurn religious "solutions" when they are experiencing dread or despair. They are not susceptible to persuasion at that point in time. To forestall people from turning to God in a crisis, they need to be persuaded before the crisis hits that immortality is an illusion and provides only the thin consolation of a false hope.

And how do we persuade people that religious promises of immortality offer only a false hope? Religion is a complex phenomenon and religious belief has many causes, which may differ from individual to individual. Surely, however, critical examination of beliefs in immortality and the evidence offered in support of such beliefs have contributed to increased skepticism. As indicated in my opening paragraph, criticism of religion is often labeled "negative" and contrasted with the so-called positive aspects of the humanist outlook. This is a false dichotomy based on semantics and word play. Eliminating false hopes and helping ensure that a person's beliefs reflect reality is as "positive" an activity as anything else. Moreover, critical examination of religion is an indispensable element of the humanist outlook. One cannot begin to develop a naturalistic perspective on life until all illusions relating to the supernatural are stripped away.

Humanist hope is grounded in reality. That is both its limitation and its strength. We cannot wish away the finality of death or other irretrievable losses. Nor can we provide acceptable answers to those who demand wish fulfillment. But if we have achieved the understanding that religion and belief in immortality are illusions, we can resist the temptation to yield to wishful thinking at times of crisis. With our gaze firmly fixed on the facts of reality, we can appreciate what life can and cannot offer—and that will be true whether we have the limitless horizons of a Faust or the more prosaic opportunities of an ordinary individual.

Ronald A. Lindsay is president and CEO of the Center for Inquiry and of the Council for Secular Humanism.

THE LABYRINTH: GOD, DARWIN, AND THE MEANING OF LIFE

Philip Appleman

The simpler the society, the cruder the problems: we can imagine Neanderthals crouching in fear—of the tiger, of the dark, of thunder—but we do not suppose they had the leisure for exquisite neuroses.

We have changed all that. Replete with leisure time and creature comforts but nervously dependent on a network of unfathomable technologies, impatient with our wayward social institutions, repeatedly betrayed by our "spiritual" leaders, and often deceived by our own extravagant hopes, we wander the labyrinth asking ourselves: What went wrong?

The answers must begin with our expectations: What is it we want? And why? What kind of people are we?

A beast condemned to be more than a beast: that is the human condition. Our anatomy, the fossil record, and our genetic blueprint all make our lineage increasingly clear. As Charles Darwin revealed to us, we are indeed half brothers to the gorilla, cousins to the other mammals, relatives of all the vertebrates (and also distant kin to corn and to corn-borers, to bacteria and to penicillin). The structure of our bones testifies to our genealogy: the hand of a human is formed on the same pattern as the hand of an orangutan, the flipper of a seal, the wing of a bat. Embryology tells us more: the human embryo is barely distinguishable from that of a tortoise or a dog or a chicken. Our DNA defines and identifies us: we share more than 98 percent of our genetic heritage with our close relative the chimpanzee.

Slowly diverging from our forebears in the course of human evolution, we gradually developed a large brain capable of making generalizations and abstractions, of theorizing, of imagining things. Half animal, half aspiration, we were never as big as a bear, as speedy as a wolf, or as powerful as a lion, but we routed all of those competitors because the large brain proved to be the ultimate weapon: it made us the supreme tool-using and arms-bearing animal. The hairy mammoth, so huge as to seem invulnerable, became our prey.

Every gain carries loss on its back. The brain that could imagine a useful tool could also imagine spiritual kingdoms and invent a "divine" creation. In this primal fiction, the human species assigned itself the role of Chosen People. The other animals, our biological family, became in this perspective mere fodder, and we presumed dominion over the fish of the sea, the fowl of the air, and every living thing that moves upon the earth.

Our loss of innocence was not because we devoured an apple; it was because we made the chauvinistic assumption that all other living things are expendable and subject to our whims. Once lost, innocence cannot be recovered. It remains to be seen whether maturity or wisdom can replace it; as a species, we have hardly ever tested those qualities.

Divine right is a convenient argument for imperialists. *Deus vult*, "God wills it," serves not only aggressor nations but aggressor species, too. The human assault on the plant and animal kingdoms has always been based on the explicit or implicit assumption of divine authority—an assumption so arrogant and so dissociated from reality that it is inherently unstable and self-destructive.

Clinging to our "divine" prerogatives, we cannot avoid that devastation: in our fantasies of godlike superiority are the seeds of neurosis; and when they bear their dragon fruit, we run for the mind-healers.

The mind-healers instruct us in what we already know: that we begin our lives in total helplessness but with boundless desire; that our dependency, and therefore this inner contradiction, persists for many years; that we cannot escape this dilemma unless we develop a sense of objective reality and a willingness to postpone desire, to limit our craving, and to channel our energies in useful, or anyway socially acceptable, activities. We have to acknowledge that there is a world of living things around us deserving our attention and respect.

If we cannot make that adjustment to external reality, we fall prey to anxiety, a straitjacket that restricts our ability to make reasonable choices. Then the unreal becomes our reality, and we grope our way through that labyrinth pursued by the terrors of our own imagination.

The large brain is the ultimate weapon, and sometimes it is aimed at us. We are capable of abstractions and of imagining things; that is part of the problem. We imagine all sorts of useful and pleasant things: wheels, shoes, poems. But the imagination refuses to stop before it is too late and proceeds to invent sinister hells, sumptuous heavens, and miscellaneous hypotheses like "God."

God is an unnecessary hypothesis, but for many people suffering the terrors of the imagination, it is a seductive one. People in general have never exhibited much passion for the disciplined pursuit of knowledge, but they are always tempted by easy answers. God is an easy answer.

Why are we here? Where will we spend eternity? The brain has become capable of inventing questions to which there are no satisfactory answers. For such questions, God is a convenience: the unanswerable question is referred to the undefinable being, and lo, we have the impression of an answer, though in fact we know no more than before. This seems to soothe some minds temporarily, as an empty bottle may soothe a crying baby; the nourishment from each is the same. *God* is a term that deliberately masks our ignorance.

Whenever God is invoked, language and sense part company. For that very reason, God has practical and political uses that partly account for its survival as a hypothesis. Among its other conveniences, God has always comforted aggressors by blessing the carnage of battle: armies carry their own chaplains. God is described as that which knows everything and is all-powerful. If so, then there is no escaping the conclusion that God is ultimately responsible for everything that happens: for the Holocaust, for the carpet-bombing of primitive villages, for the defilement of children, for slavery. Priests have been on hand to sanction all of those activities: God is a serviceable bureaucrat.

The worship of the undefinable is necessarily illogical: "Praise the mercy and goodness of God for saving my life," says the survivor of an earthquake in which God, with complete indifference, has just brushed away a thousand lives.

The large brain, that masterpiece of evolution capable of wonder but unpracticed in reasoning, throws patterns across the stars: Aquarius, Taurus, Capricorn. To invent these images is poetry; to believe in them is faith. God's survival depends upon our peopling the heavens with angels and archangels, chimeras of our banal imagination. No wonder the prophets thundered against the sin of knowledge, the sin of pride: God depends upon our ignorance as much as any magician.

Learning is hard work; imagining is easy. Given our notorious capacity for indolence, is it any wonder that school is so unpopular, faith so attractive? So we fumble through the labyrinth of our lives, making believe that we have heard answers to our questions, even to our prayers; and yet, deep down, we know that something is out of joint, has always been out of joint. How long? we lament. How long, O Lord?

The only answer from the clouds is that the Lord thy God is a jealous God. And that's not all. God is also, judging from his own written record, vindictive, tyrannical, narcissistic, bloodthirsty, bigoted, and irresponsible. It is hard to imagine why anyone would want to be cast in that image. And yet so powerful are the urges of anxiety and neurosis that people quite seriously wish to emulate this moral aberration. Why should that be?

Recall that the essential characteristics of the infant's personality are selfishness and boundless desire. To grow out of infancy and childhood, it is necessary to adjust to the reality of the outer world, which inevitably means limiting our desires in accordance with conditions in that real world around us. That's straightforward enough.

Throughout that real world, though, are embedded the booby traps of theology. The most dangerous of these is the seductive promise of an eternity of infinite delight—just what we have been painstakingly weaned away from since our infantile years. Now, once again, the priests deliberately tempt us with

THE SCIENTIFIC EXAMINATION OF RELIGION | 117

these blandishments, exhort us to desire eternal bliss, and persuade us to feel guilty if we do not.

And yet there is no guarantee that we'll ever get that grand prize, because the distributor of the awards is the same capricious tyrant who flatly refused to explain cosmic justice even to one of his favorites, Job, and who informs us that eternal delight is his to distribute as he sees fit, quite apart from our merits and according to a whimsical quality called "grace." God either gives grace and rewards us for having it or withholds grace and punishes us for lacking it. Even Las Vegas casinos give better odds than that.

No wonder, then, that religion, in pandering to our infantile wishes, leaves us unfit for dealing with reality. No wonder that under such pressures so many people become confused and ill, believing they are something they are not. No wonder they are so often reduced to a state of primitive anguish, calling for help to the barren stars.

The fact is that religion is not simply a maladaptive factor in our lives; it was specifically designed by its various priesthoods to be maladaptive, charging us to abjure "this world." Attention to an afterlife necessarily reduces our interest in this life, but the problem goes deeper than that: the glittering image of paradise breeds actual contempt for "this world."

So in terms of our personal maturity, the dream of heaven is an outright affliction. Given a fair chance, this life can be well worth living, but in the context of infinite rewards, our small struggles and occasional victories on this blue-green planet always seem like petty stuff. Under the crystalline dome of our medieval theological heaven, life becomes a hothouse that nourishes frustration and neurosis.

Some examples are in order. Consider the religious people

we have known all our lives. Consider history. Consider the daily news.

In the U.S. Army during World War II and afterward in the Merchant Marine, I encountered many curious notions. One of my army buddies once solemnly advised me that I could cure my "weak eyes" (i.e., myopia) by washing them in urine, and a Merchant Marine watchmate insisted that "Some people would be real sons of bitches if it wasn't for religion."

The seaman who pronounced that bit of piety was, to my firsthand knowledge, a drunk, a liar, a cheat, and an adulterer. Perhaps he thought of these qualities as his perverse credentials for setting moral standards, the seagoing equivalent of the opinionated bald barber or the arrogant, cigarette-smoking doctor. As I enumerate the liars, cheats, and lechers I have known personally, I realize that most of them were conventional believers, whereas my agnostic and atheist friends are mostly honest, kindly, generous, and clean-living.

We may account for this divergent behavior partly on the assumption that religious people can "afford" to be immoral: all they need to do to exonerate themselves from sin, immorality, and undetected crime is to ask forgiveness—rather like the goddess Venus, who revirginized herself after every orgy. If God exists, the old saying should go, then anything is permissible.

Nonreligious people have no such easy out. Their moral accountability is not to some whimsical spirit in the sky, famous for easy absolutions such as three Hail Marys and ten seconds of contrition. They must account to themselves and live with their own conduct; they cannot shift their shortcomings onto God's shoulders. Therefore, they have to be more careful about making mistakes, and this leads naturally to an acute sensitivity to the plight of their fellow human beings. The social instincts, said the agnostic Charles Darwin, lead naturally to the golden rule.

Another way to account for the morality of unbelievers is that they are less perverted by the antisocial tendencies of religious thinking, including the seductions of fanaticism. Some people professed astonishment at the religious mania of nine hundred devotees of the Reverend Jim Jones, falling face down in Guyana in a mass suicide-murder. And yet that act was a testimony to the very essence of religion: a wholeheartedly sincere belief in a personal redeemer.

In Iran, after the Shah was dethroned, his priestly successors sent thousands to their deaths by kangaroo court and firing squads: that was an act of religious fervor, proudly affirmed as such by its perpetrators.

These are by no means isolated or unusual occurrences. To the fanatical mind, the act of pure religion has always been an act of pure violence: the hanging of "witches" by pious Protestants; the massacres of Huguenots, Albigensians, Incas, and Aztecs by pious Catholics; the starvation of Armenians by pious Muslims; the slaughter of Midianites, Amalekites, and Philistines by pious Hebrews; and the slaughter of Jews by pious Christians throughout two thousand years of "Western civilization."

And of course that characteristic religious fanaticism continues and accelerates today, so that in recent years we have witnessed all of the following:

- Catholics killing Protestants (and vice versa) in Ireland
- Christians killing Muslims (and vice versa) in Lebanon
- Muslims killing Hindus (and vice versa) in India
- Hindus killing Buddhists (and vice versa) in Sri Lanka
- Jews killing Muslims (and vice versa) in Palestine

• Muslims killing Christians (and vice versa) in Egypt, Algeria, Azerbaijan, Indonesia, and Nigeria
• Roman Catholics killing Orthodox Christians (and vice versa) in the former Yugoslavia—and both of them killing Muslims (and vice versa)
• Sunni Muslims killing Shiites (and vice versa) in Iraq, and Shiites killing Baha'is in Iran
• Religious fanatics killing tourists in Egypt, unveiled teenage girls in Algiers, subway commuters in Tokyo, thousands at the World Trade Center, yeshiva students in Brooklyn, and doctors and their patients in Florida, New York, Alabama, Massachusetts, and Kansas

Religion stalks across the face of human history, knee-deep in the blood of innocents, clasping its red hands in hymns of praise to an approving God.

World history is full of accounts of fanatical ideologies careening toward human tragedy, but rarely has there been a more forceful demonstration of the disastrous effects of religious ideologies than at this moment. And yet, in the midst of a worldwide bloodbath in the name of religion, Americans are being relentlessly bullied into an uncritical deference to religion by their clerical and political shamans. High-powered censorship campaigns by well-financed religious groups constantly assault our writers, artists, teachers, and musicians and our schools, libraries, films, books, and magazines.

There is also a very personal side to what we must consider "the religion problem." When we begin to think of our recent roster of ministers of religion, those "holy men," we encounter a veritable Chaucerian gallery of rogues and felons. For we now have seen:

• the Reverend Jim Bakker imprisoned for fraud and conspiracy
• the Reverend Jimmy Swaggart humiliated in sex scandals and in violation of federal tax laws
• the Ayatollah Khomeini and his successors lusting for the blood of a writer
• his holiness the pope obstructing birth control programs in hungry, vastly overpopulated nations
• Rabbi Meir Kahane making a political career out of religious hatreds
• the Reverend Sun Myung Moon imprisoned for tax evasion
• 162 televangelists under investigation for financial irregularities
• thousands of Roman Catholic priests charged with sexual abuse, child molestation, indecent assault, corruption of minors, and sexual battery

As a certain prophet once said, "By their fruits ye shall know them." To believe that religion keeps people from being "sons of bitches" is about as sensible as believing that a good washing in urine will cure your weak eyes.

But it is not by their deeds that the world's religions wish to be judged—or usually *are* judged. The most outrageous "religious" behavior is always absorbed into the spongy justification of means-to-a-good-end, and it is never the victims of persecution and fanaticism who hold the attention of the faithful; it is the towering cathedral, soaring rhetoric, and official parades of good intentions. This perversion of perspective is the triumph of The Ultimate Organization.

Priesthoods begin in vision and prophecy: sometimes benevolent, sometimes cruel, but always somehow "spiritual"—the product of some personal insight. Eventually, however, priesthoods follow the trend of all civilized life, getting themselves organized and losing their personal nature, whereupon the original vision fades or becomes distorted, and The Organization itself becomes the object of self-preservation, aggrandizing itself in monumental buildings, pompous rituals, mazes of rules and regulations, and a relentless grinding toward autocracy.

None of the other priesthoods have managed all this as successfully as the early Christian clergy, which expediently allied itself with the secular powers and modeled its own structure after the most successful empire of its time, complete with top-to-bottom control and a self-selecting, self-perpetuating bureaucracy. Thus the "Roman" church created for itself a kind of secular immortality sustained by a tight network of binding regulations, rigid hierarchies, and local fiefdoms, which people are born or are coerced or seduced into—and then find that confining maze almost impossible to escape from.

But with that pervasive and aggressive organization came the attendant problems. Small organizations may make small mistakes; large ones are in constant danger of making catastrophic mistakes, nationwide and continentwide errors, vast programs of wrongheadedness and social depredation, all enforced by their organizational efficiency. So we look back and see the murderous "Christian" Crusades with their millions of innocent victims; we see the centuries of European Catholic/Protestant wars leaving behind vast landscapes of death and devastation; we see compliance in and justification for genocide against the American Indians; we see mainstream religious support for the institution of human slavery; and we see the brutal religious repression of valuable human knowledge by burning scientists at the stake or threatening them with barbaric tortures.

In our own time, the Roman Catholic Church has made the gravest error of all: setting its worldwide power and influence against the clear and urgent need for sensible population limitation. Largely because of that influence, human populations are now well beyond the carrying capacity of the earth and are rapidly expanding, especially in the poorest countries. As a direct result, we see increasingly devastating human misery: hunger, malnutrition, starvation, poverty, illness, illiteracy, joblessness, and homelessness—not to mention the consequent degradation of our environment and the destruction of countless other species who used to share this planet with us.

In the midst of all this social and moral wreckage, the priests try to maintain a facade of "doing good," repeating their protestations of love and charity—all while their real activities are wrecking human lives and human hopes on a vast scale. There is a word for this kind of activity, talking about love while blighting people's lives: it is *hypocrisy.*

Consider the fruits of hypocrisy: if we truly believed we were being audited daily for an account in heaven and that faith and good works were the outward and visible signs of grace, then of course the uses of this world would seem weary, stale, flat, and unprofitable, and we would turn our full attention to acts of piety. There would be little interest then in such homely satisfactions as good work or good cooking or good tennis. The arts would be viewed as trivial amusements or as temptations of the devil, and music and poetry would wither away for lack of interest. Love would be chastened and sex abjured for fear of irreverent fervor. Weeds would grow up in the cracks of the human spirit.

Fortunately, such consequences rarely occur in real life, because most of the people who give lip service to religion retain a healthy skepticism about it. This is the benevolent face of hypocrisy. Except perhaps for a few cloistered individuals, nobody these days sacrifices many things of this world for the alleged glories of the afterlife, although gurus and holy books exhort us all to do so—and indeed if we were truly counting on an eternal reward, that would make sense. No earthly pleasure, not even a romantic dinner or a Shakespeare sonnet or a painting by Cézanne, is worth the risk of losing heaven. Yet few people are abjuring the world; we are taking the cash and letting the credit go. So much the better.

The trouble is, some of us can't seem to stop worrying about an afterlife that we don't really believe in, and as a result the toadstools of neurosis spring up in the dank labyrinth of our psyches. On the one hand, when we momentarily break free from the snaky coils of childhood teachings, we find ourselves fretting about our apostasy. On the other hand, when we sheepishly return to orthodox reverence, our self-respect is automatically diminished, and we regret the opportunities for personal growth and adventure that we are missing.

Most of us need to be much tougher-minded, more resolute in rejecting the bribes of the afterlife. Once definitely done with our adolescent longing for the Absolute, we would find this world valuable after all—and poignantly valuable precisely because it is not eternal. Doomed to extinction, our loves, our work, our friendships, our tastes are all painfully precious. We look about us, on the streets and in the subways, and discover that we are beautiful because we are mortal, priceless because we are so rare in the universe and so fleeting. Whatever we are, whatever we make of ourselves, is all we will ever have—and that, in its profound simplicity, is the meaning of life.

Evolving from an earthy past, from a family line that was hairy, tailed, and arboreal, how can we presume to ponder the meaning of life? Yet the large brain is a restless organ, and it will not stop asking questions, even presumptuous ones.

We are equipped with abstractions, with imagination. The trick is to use these sharp tools without getting hurt. When they help us to understand the world as it is, we must be grateful. When they create destructive fantasies, we must be on guard. According to the old holy books and the old philosophies, we were designed by benevolent gods. Darwin showed, on the contrary, that we are the product of war, famine, and death. Pre-Darwinian philosophies were constructed on false premises and are therefore basically flawed.

Ever since Darwin we have known that we came this way not by design but by random variation and the directive natural forces of selection and adaptation. To go on looking for design around us, outside us, is a destructive fantasy. It prohibits maturity.

And yet design is one of our fondest imaginings, and we will not abandon it. If it doesn't exist outside ourselves, we will create it inside, in our work and our loves, in our art and our avocations. This is not a trivial endeavor: we stake our happiness on it. We create the abstraction of love beyond sex and can, with difficulties, be faithful to it. We entertain the notion of truth and set out to test it. We imagine freedom and try to achieve it. We are able to control these designs because we have constructed them and set their rules.

If we come to maturity by recognizing what is outside us, we come to wisdom by knowing what is inside. Balancing our desires and aspirations, orchestrating our responses to the world we encounter and our initiatives to the world we create, we teach ourselves all we will ever know about the meaning of life.

To presume to understand the meaning of life—what arrogance! Just look in a mirror: we are all dying animals, flyspecks on history. Our lives are a speeded-up film, jerkily passing from childhood to maturity to decrepitude to death: the career of a mayfly.

So a philosophy of life must account for death, and so should a psychology of life. To the other animals, death is an accident. Our large brain makes it a tragedy, and tragedy calls for reasons: Why? Why me? And reasons indeed the large brain has, reasons the heart does not know.

Some of them are make-believe, the mumbo-jumbo of theologians; some are other kinds of wishful thinking. But now we are after the truth, nothing but the truth, and this is how it begins: once upon a time, in the cosmic neighborhood of our galaxy, a vast cloud of dust and gases condensed into a mass so hot and so dense that it became a huge thermonuclear reactor—a star. In its gravitational field smaller condensations became planets, and on at least one of these, after it cooled, primitive oceans formed, providing conditions that could subsequently bring forth organic compounds, then molecules, then primitive cells. Some of these eventually began to photosynthesize, and entities were then well on their way to a splendid proliferation that later, by the process of natural selection, became ferns, conifers, herbs, and flowers and also reptiles, birds, insects, and mammals—including us.

As the orderly processes of nature go their ways, genetic discrepancies frequently occur in living things: blips on the screen of uniformity. They are almost always maladaptive and quickly suppressed. Out of many discrepancies, occasionally one is useful or opportunistic, and new characteristics thus enter the gene pool. A dozen or a hundred or a thousand more, and then another accretion: that is how we crept all the way from photosynthetic algae to oxygen-breathing primates.

Nowhere along the way was any all-powerful creator needed to step in and shape things. The process has always run itself and goes on running itself. So here we stand, after billions of years of stability and billions of years of change: human beings, upright and cerebral, capable of anything, the most admirable and despicable animal on Earth, making symphonies and sadism, medicine and malice. With *Homo sapiens*, a wild card is loose in the deck. We invent names for it: consciousness, intelligence, free will. Like a sub-atomic particle, it is impossible to observe in a pure, unaltered state, but we realize that it is there: we think, therefore we are.

Knowing what we know, suspecting what we suspect about the compelling determinations of our genes and the stern persuasions of our culture, how do we square all this logically with the odd notion of free will? By recognizing that there are no absolutes in nature. A totally persuasive environment is a fairy tale of the mind. The large brain can imagine a hermetic prison of the environment, but in the real world there are too many cracks in the structure of our conditioning to permit it to be a prison for the imagination. We imagine ourselves free, and therefore, within unknown limits, we are free.

We will never know precisely what those limits are. You see, says the mind, you are trapped in your labyrinth. You see, says the imagination, you are free. Both are correct. The Absolute has turned its back.

With that understanding, we can come to terms with the irreducible fact of death.

Charles Darwin, after many years of hard work and illness, controversy and honor, lay on his deathbed. A biographer tells us: "During the night of April 18th [1882], about a quarter to twelve, he had a severe attack and passed into a faint, from which he was brought back to consciousness with great difficulty. He seemed to recognize the approach of death, and said, 'I am not the least afraid to die.'" Those were his last words.

Living among the relentless Victorian pieties, educated to be a clergyman, surrounded by threats of literal burning hellfire: Why didn't Darwin fear death? Part of the answer is that by the time he was a mature man, he simply knew too much about the real world to be frightened by superstitions. The once-orthodox Cambridge undergraduate had, he said, "gradually come . . . to see that the Old Testament, from its manifestly false history of the world, with the Tower of Babel, the rainbow as a sign, etc., etc., and from its attributing to God the feelings of a revengeful tyrant, was no more to be trusted than the sacred books of the Hindoos or the beliefs of any barbarian."

Another reason Darwin didn't fear death and hellfire is that he could not take seriously religious threats that were openly sadistic. "I can indeed hardly see how anyone ought to wish Christianity to be true: for if so the plain language of the text seems to show that [those] who do not believe, and this would include my Father, Brother, and almost all my best friends, will be everlastingly punished. . . . And this is a damnable doctrine."

Throughout his adult life, Darwin took a deep human satisfaction in his important work, in the comradeship of his friends, and in the love of his family. That was enough, and he was not merely content with it; ill though he often was, he was a happy man.

And he was not afraid to die.

Death, Darwin knew, is simply a natural part of a natural process. Death is always out there, waiting: only its timing is in doubt. Eventually we will have played our small part in the great system of nature and passed on, leaving the system intact. We are, we have always been, a part of nature in the same way tigers or termites are.

Priests and preachers in most religions refuse to accept this sensible view of things. "Eternal Life," they cry—thus thwarting all hope of a mature personal philosophy. By promising glory in a glittering but unreal eternity, they sour our satisfactions in a brief but genuine present. They portray a God who supposedly plans all things reasonably and wisely. After all, if we are reasonable, surely God must be supremely reasonable. Our bodies, we are told, are temples, so we treat them with respect and look forward to our threescore and ten years.

But God, it turns out, has something else in mind for us, and eventually we find out that God is not only whimsical but also a vandal. After years of our taking good care of our tidy little temples, God suddenly and without explanation breaks down the door, smashes the windows, rips the paintings, and slashes the furniture. All of our lives we have been prudent: about diet, about drinking and smoking, about doing everything in moderation—and all of a sudden, without any warning at all, God shrieks in our ear: Cancer!

But what if you are not religious when cancer slips up without warning, threatening death? You do not fear death any more than Darwin did, but you hate it. You hate the loss, and the sorrow of leaving behind bereaved family and friends. So in your mind, and in the minds of those who love you, there is a sharp pain, a conscious rage at being mortal. Ants and alligators must also die, but they do not face that fact with rage or regret; those feelings are human.

Religion says: console yourself, there will be another

chance, another life. Two things are wrong with this: first, there is not a shred of evidence for it; second, it is a sop, consciously intended to blunt our rage and regret, thus dehumanizing us. Our anger at death is precious, testifying to the value of life; our sorrow for family and friends testifies to our devotion. Every noble quality we possess depends for its poignant value on our natural brevity. Our final pain is mortal, and our own; we will not have it cheapened by the seductions of an alleged immortality.

Face to face with death, we realize: the meaning of life is inside our lives, not outside them. We cannot impose on our experience a meaningfulness that we have not ourselves built into it. Our true philosophy of life is whatever we choose to do from moment to moment. If we regularly behave honestly and decently to those around us, then our philosophy is clearly a healthy and adaptive one, accounting for our lives in terms of our whole social environment. The sum total of our actions at a given time constitutes our philosophy of life.

Darwin on his deathbed could look back at forty-three years of devotion to a loving wife and forty-five years of devotion to a grand idea. At the end, he had one characteristic regret: that he could not somehow have lived two lives so that one could have been spent in full-time philanthropic work. The mind is tyrannically ambitious: the flesh cannot keep pace with it. Still, Darwin was content; he had made his commitments, and he had kept them.

If the meaning of life is simply the fabric of our whole existence, then no wonder our brief careers seem to us so illogically precious, so worth clinging to. Self-preservation: Even at the molecular level, is there a kind of self-interest in all that nonstop microscopic scurrying? Certainly at the level of the amoeba there is, and "up" through the scale of living things; it's always there, the fundamental imperative of life: survival. Preachers may sneer at this, but notice: they continue to pass the collection plate.

If we are to make any sense of what we call "moral principles," we have to begin with the basic Darwinian fact of self-preservation. At all levels of animal life, this of course means looking out for number one; but at "higher" biological levels (not to mention the ants, wolves, and other "social animals"), self-preservation also means extending our perceptions of survival beyond the individual: to the family, to the clan, to the tribe. At a certain stage of our social development, it becomes possible—indeed essential—for people to see that a more effective conception of self-interest includes wider and wider circles of mutual interest: the nation, the continent, the world. At that stage, we come to understand that our personal well-being is substantially dependent on the well-being of people we have never seen and never will.

But even at "primitive" levels of social understanding, human beings (no doubt including proto-humans for millions and millions of years) have recognized that in order to live together in communities—as people must, in order to survive—we have to have some basic mutual understandings, tacit or explicit, some ground rules by which we try to abide. As Darwin observed, these always come down to a kind of golden rule: treat others as you would like to be treated. This very basic idea was undoubtedly worked out, evolved, as a social necessity, a practical understanding independent of mystical insights; its virtually worldwide acknowledgment makes it certain that it is not the unique property of any one culture, much less of any one religion.

Darwin was often successful in his hunches, not because he

was lucky but because he knew so much, worked so hard, thought so long and so clearly, and was so smart. Thinking about our social ground rules, he surmised that after millions of years of living together in communities, our social behavior might be to some extent inherited. Darwin called it "social instinct," the inheritance from our long past not only of the self-preservation imperative, the so-called animalistic urges that often make people extraordinarily selfish and even ruthless, but also our tendencies for "good" social behavior: showing respect for others, fair dealing, honesty—and, by a natural extension, kindness and charitableness. If Darwin was right about that hunch, then we all must "intuitively" recognize basic "right" from basic "wrong" in any given circumstance; that innate awareness is perhaps the foundation of what we call "conscience." But even if it turns out that Darwin was wrong, we would nevertheless be obliged to pass along, as part of our collective social experience, those same tendencies.

Once our species had evolved to social consciousness and communal morality, people naturally began to express their social approval with praise and to enforce their disapproval with contempt, anger, and ostracism. The gravest social offenses required sterner measures, so societies everywhere had to prohibit them by custom, taboo, and law, with penalties for violators. The social policing of community ethics thus would have begun as a secular necessity, not as a religious function. By the time the talented Cro-Magnon artists painted the caves at Lascaux, those moral sanctions had no doubt long since been part of our evolutionary inheritance—tens of thousands of years before the Bible, before the Vedas, before the Dhammapada, the Zend-Avesta, or the Qur'an.

But as a famous atheist once said, "If there were no God, it would be necessary to invent one." And of course we did: that is when our big problems began. Evolution on this planet is billions of years older than religion; but when religion finally came along, thousands of years after evolution had developed our social instincts, it co-opted our socially evolved good impulses and encumbered them with a myriad of disparate, controversial, and contradictory gods, priesthoods, scriptures, myths, and dogmas.

Of course, we also retained our so-called animal instincts, right along with our highly evolved social instincts, and some people have always been motivated more by their primitive than by their evolved natures. When religions preempted the job of disciplining such antisocial people, they tried to deal with them both by the promise of heaven and by the threat of hell. But neither of those sanctions has ever worked very well, which is why (among other things) totally immersed Southern Baptists always performed the lynchings for the Ku Klux Klan, nice Catholic boys have always run the Mafia, a devout Jew murdered his peace-loving prime minister, and in a notorious American election, pious white church-going Christians voted 2 to 1 for a declared Nazi. After five thousand years of Judaic Jeremiads and two thousand years of Christian polemics, we find ourselves in what some people choose to call a "Christian nation," where the prisons are crowded with obdurate felons, most of whom believe in God.

The problem is not that antisocial people don't know what's right and wrong or good and bad. As Darwin suggested, they may even have inherited that knowledge; in any case, it is all taught and reinforced by our laws, by families, and by schools. The problem is not that they don't know but that they don't care. Consider this opinion: "The earth is degenerating in these latter days. Bribery and corruption abound. Children no longer obey their parents, and it is evident that the end of the world is rapidly approaching." That is from an Assyrian tablet about five thou-

sand years old—but similar laments are common throughout
recorded history and under every political and religious regime.
Clearly a perennial question must be: How can people be taught,
or encouraged, to *care* about right and wrong? If not simply by
precept then perhaps by example?

Our social and political leaders, given their professed religiosity, might be expected to be inspiring social role models,
but they have often failed in that service. This is partly because
the economic and political systems they represent and embody
have customarily been patterned not on our evolved social instincts—our evolutionary golden rule—but on our more primitive survival instincts. Most of us understand that our survival
cannot be a matter of simply eat-or-be-eaten; our survival depends upon widening our circle of mutual support. But opportunistic politicians and feral businessmen have almost always
set our social tone and social standards, so it is no surprise that
our evolved social instincts are so often overwhelmed by primitive selfishness and a callous disregard for the less fortunate.
As La Rochefoucauld observed, we all have enough strength to
bear the misfortunes of others. Clearly some other role models
are needed. Let us look again to science.

We are always moralists, Dr. Johnson said, but only occasionally
mathematicians. It is usually assumed that science, strictly
speaking, has no ethics, that the gap between what is and what
ought to be is broad and unbridgeable. But our ethics, whatever
its source, can hardly emerge from a vacuum of knowledge; in
fact our knowledge often tempers our ethical inclinations.
Scientific knowledge has at the bare minimum a selective ethical function, identifying false issues that we can reasonably ignore—imagined astrological influences on our moral decisions,

for instance. Science offers us the opportunity of basing our ethical choices on factual data and true relationships rather than on misconceptions or superstitions; that must be considered a valuable service.

Beyond that selective function, biological information has often been directly used (and misused) to support various types of ethical thinking. Unscrupulous people have sometimes appealed to spurious readings of scientific data in order to bulwark their arguments; that is what happened to Darwinism when Nazis perverted it in an attempt to legitimize their racist ideology. It is an understandable wariness of this kind of perversion that heats up the disputes about race, gender, and intelligence today.

More characteristically, though, the growth of scientific knowledge has tended to have socially progressive implications. Factual knowledge of the physical world has on the whole been a better basis for human understanding, human solidarity, and human sympathy than were folklore or superstition. The old myth-supported notions of tribal and racial supremacy have been superseded, at least among the educated, by the biological knowledge that we are one people, one species, in one world.

Finally, the scientific temper of mind is itself of service to moralists, sometimes supplementary to and sometimes superior to, our social instincts. It is the "objective" scientists, these days, who are often in the vanguard of ethical thought; they are, for instance, enlarging our understanding of the capacities of the higher mammals and of our moral responsibilities with respect to them. The fascinating work of Jane Goodall and others with primate societies in Africa has not only broadened our knowledge of primate behavior, but it has, in the process, illuminated the kinship of humans and the other animals. Human beings, proud of the role of *Homo faber*, the creative animal, the toolmaker, now have to share this role with the clever chimps who, we have now learned, also have a distinct sense of self, a consciousness of individual personality. No wonder scientists are beginning to ask, quite seriously, as Carl Sagan did, questions like "If chimpanzees have consciousness, if they are capable of abstractions, do they not have what until now has been described as 'human rights'? How smart does a chimpanzee have to be before killing him constitutes murder?"

There may be no absolute values in ethics, but there are relative values in the various existing ethical systems; one could make a persuasive case that those systems that are not only the most altruistic but also sensitive to the broadest constituencies are, by virtue of those qualities, superior to the others. Richard Dawkins writes, "If I say that I am more interested in preventing the slaughter of large whales than I am in improving housing conditions for people, I am likely to shock some of my friends." And he adds, "Whether the ethic of 'speciesism' . . . can be put on a logical footing any more sound that that of 'racism,' I do not know. What I do know is that it has no proper basis in evolutionary biology."

Our arrogant primal fiction cast the whole human race in the role of Chosen People and reduced all other living things to fodder, subject to our whims. With a growing recognition among biologists of the ugly and self-defeating aspects of that archaic speciesism, we may have reason to foresee a future consensus that a narrowly species-centered ethics is inadequate, not so much to our emotions (which have almost always failed us in this matter) but to our reason, now under instruction by new biological perceptions.

In the truly well-balanced human being (that will-o'-the-wisp of utopian thought), reason and emotion would be always in harmony, indeed in symbiotic function. In the meantime, it is reassuring to discover that biologists, engaged in "objective" research, so often become passionate about their work and about the world it affects. Our cautious and rational perception of truth, it appears, sometimes causes, and sometimes is served by, moral fervor.

None of this would be so evident or so pertinent to our lives if biology were not a science so thoroughly unified by the principle of evolution as to afford philosophical perspectives of its own. We owe that unification, of course, to Charles Darwin. Evolution by natural selection continues to serve biologists in their professional work and to inspire them to earnest pondering about our place in the universe; some of the wisest thinkers writing about the human condition today are biologists.

Could it be that a fuller, broader understanding of our biological condition might encourage people to care about right and wrong? "The moral faculties," Darwin wrote in *The Descent of Man*, "are generally and justly esteemed as of higher value than the intellectual powers. But we should bear in mind that the activity of the mind . . . is one of the fundamental though secondary bases of conscience. This affords the strongest argument for educating and stimulating in all possible ways the intellectual faculties of every human being."

"Many things are at hand," wrote Pope Gregory the Great in 601 C.E., "wars, famines, plagues, earthquakes . . . [but] let not your mind be in any way disturbed; for these [are but] signs of the end of the world." In other words, wars, famines, and plagues are not social problems demanding solutions but only ineluctable divine retribution, which makes the other face of religious escapism social irresponsibility. "God's will" becomes a thin mask for social cynicism.

Writing twelve hundred years later, Charles Darwin supplied an unintentional gloss on that pope's remark: "To those who fully admit the immortality of the human soul, the destruction of our world will not appear so dreadful."

The diversions of the Romans were bread and circuses; in our time they are sensational crime, sporting events, the sexual behavior of celebrities, and religious escapism. Nourished on such pap, many people find themselves lost in the labyrinth of neurosis and succumb to easy answers and seductive promises. The priests need not soon fear for their jobs.

Those rare women and men who seriously ponder our own dark ages rarely have illusions about converting the masses to rigorous thought; the poor in spirit have always been with us and will surely be with us for a long, long time. Short of any quick conversions, though, there is still a value in the ranks of thoughtful people speaking out and testifying, for only an utterly hopeless cynic would surrender the distant future along with the present. Every small light in the pervading darkness, from Giordano Bruno and Galileo to Thomas Paine and Charles Darwin and to Margaret Sanger and Elizabeth Cady Stanton, is valuable and necessary. Like characters in a perpetual Chekhov drama, we can imagine a more enlightened future age looking back on our time with distaste and incredulity but nevertheless acknowledging those voices in our wilderness who kept the Enlightenment alive until humanity in general became worthy of it.

The history of law in the West, after all, records our gradual transition away from the traditional religious resort to vengeance and toward a secular and humanistic confidence in reason and social equity; away from religion-sponsored vindictiveness (an eye for an eye) and toward the secular and humanistic reasonableness of non-cruel and non-unusual punishment; away from centuries of religion-sanctioned human slavery and toward the secular and humanistic ideals of freedom of speech, thought, and belief; away from religion-sponsored "blue laws" that required barbarous punishment for trivial offenses and toward the secular and humanistic standard of due process in all things legal; away from the Islamic practice of chopping off the hands of thieves or the Christian practice of burning heretics alive and toward the secular and humanistic goal of separation of church and state, so that the one may not tyrannize over, exploit, or directly manipulate the other, as they always had before the humanistic Enlightenment changed things in the West.

Contrary to the popular cliché, we can and do "legislate morality" in our secular state: it is, for example, both immoral and illegal in most circumstances to kill, to steal, to embezzle, to lie under oath, to rape, or to abuse children. Although various religions proscribe many other offenses as well, our society has not felt all of them sufficiently grave or sufficiently public to warrant legal penalties. The above examples of moral legislation, however, have broad social support, and their moral imperatives are therefore enforced by the police and the criminal courts.

For a law of any sort to be effective, what is minimally necessary is a general awareness of its correctness, its evenhandedness, and its necessity. Attempts to regulate our personal habits by law have had varying fortunes. The attempt to prohibit traffic in liquor failed in this country because there was not a sufficient conviction on the part of the public that drinking was significantly harmful to anyone but the drinker (except when the drinker is driving, which is universally illegal). On the other hand, recent attempts to regulate smokers have been more successful because of the accumulating evidence of harm to others.

As long as laws are reasonable and arrived at democratically, most people will tend to obey them even when they know they can get away with breaking them: not killing, not stealing, not even running stoplights are all normally taken for granted. No matter how reasonable a law seems to some people, however, it will not be honored by all unless the society that sponsors it offers fairness and opportunity. "The law in its majestic equality," wrote Anatole France, "forbids the rich as well as the poor to sleep under bridges, to beg in the streets, and to steal bread." Millionaires do not commonly rob candy stores or push drugs on street corners; their offenses are of a more rarefied order. But as long as there is a permanent underclass, a substantial body of people who cannot find a way of sharing in the fruits of society, that underclass will always be a threat to the social fabric because, although human beings can, in difficult times, tolerate hardship, they will not accept flagrant unfairness indefinitely; an aggrieved underclass will always be trying to "get even." Given that condition, there is obviously no hope of the religious mechanisms ("Be good, and society will improve") working well in the long run; they will only serve to breed more neurosis. What is required is a secular solution, which works the other way round: "Improve the society and most people will behave better."

It is never possible to write all of the next century's laws; our consciousness of social necessity is constantly changing, and in the course of social evolution, we can always expect some degree of controversy and turmoil. In 1860 the major problem in this country was human slavery, a burning issue then, vehemently defended by conservatives, slave-owners, and most religious leaders. Today, no one would defend the slave-owners, and yet our current crop of conservatives is reluctant to allow advances in equity for those who have long been denied it: blacks, other minorities, and women. A generation or a century from now, people will surely think it strange and shameful that anyone should have balked at this natural evolution of rising expectations.

Advances in social equity, however slow and hard-won they may be, help to sustain what we think of as "progress" in what we think of as "virtue." Humane and liberal societies gradually come to a more sensitized understanding of the plight of the less fortunate and devise sensible ways of assisting them; the underclass then feels less trapped, becomes less confrontational, and is less motivated to break the social contract. Good law and good customs precede good behavior: practicing the golden rule turns out to be not only altruistic but also self-serving.

But an equitable and humanistic society would stimulate something much better than mere conformity to social rules. In such a society, people could be encouraged to ponder their own lives and their place in the world; to acquire full and accurate knowledge of that world, unwarped by myths and superstitions; and to assess human problems and act with reasonableness and compassion. Free from the racking fear of deprivation and from the labyrinth of brutal religious animosities, free from holy non-sense and pious bigotry, living in a climate of openness, toler-ance, and free inquiry, they would be able to create meaning and value in their lives: in the joy of learning, the joy of helping others; the joys of good health, physical activity, and sensual pleasure; the joy of honest labor; the joys of the richness of art, music, literature, and the adventures of the free mind; the joys of nature and wildlife and landscape—in short, in the ephemeral but genuine joy of the human experience.

That joy does not depend upon mysticism or dogma or priestly admonition; it is the joy of human life, here and now, unblemished by the dark shadow of whimsical forces in the sky.

Charles Darwin's example, both in his work and in his life, helps us to understand that that is the only "heaven" we will ever know. And it is the only one we need.

Distinguished Professor Emeritus at Indiana University Philip Appleman has published eight volumes of poetry, including New and Selected Poems, *1956–1996 (University of Arkansas Press, 1996); three novels, including* Apes and Angels *(Putnam, 1989); and several nonfiction books, including the widely used* Norton Critical Edition of *Darwin. His* Perfidious Proverbs and Other Poems: A Satirical Look at the Bible *will be published by Prometheus Books in July.*

FREE INQUIRY

is published bimonthly by the nonprofit
Council for Secular Humanism.
For more information or to subscribe, contact:

Council for Secular Humanism
P.O. Box 664
Amherst, NY 14226-0664 USA

716-636-7571 • www.secularhumanism.org